AF679469

Chronomutable Minutule Ecchymosis using Bathyal Neuronal Cantorianized

Sen

Chronomutable Minutule Ecchymosis using Bathyal Neuronal Cantorianized

First Edition December 2025

Copyright © 2025 Sen

Written by Sen

TABLE OF CONTENTS

CHAPTER NO.	TITLE	PAGE NO.

CHAPTER NO.	TITLE	PAGE NO.

CHAPTER NO.	TITLE	PAGE NO.

CHAPTER NO.	TITLE	PAGE NO.

CHAPTER 1

INTRODUCTION

1.1 OVERVIEW

People today experience significant stress at work and constant worry about job demands, leading many to overwork. This lifestyle has contributed to a rise in several health problems, including diabetes, vision impairment, memory decline, and reduced tolerance levels. Individuals aged 35 and above are particularly vulnerable, making it important to address their growing health concerns.

According to World Health Organization statistics, diabetes affected over 52.3 crore people globally in 2014. By 2030, nearly 9.8 crore Indians are expected to have type-2 diabetes. The number of diabetes cases continues to rise in both developed and developing nations, and in many developing countries, treatment and healthcare support remain inadequate. As a result, diabetic individuals face a significantly higher risk of vision-related complications—studies show that they are up to 25 times more likely to experience vision loss compared to non-diabetic individuals. The eyes are among the most vital organs in the human body. Good eyesight is essential for daily functioning and overall quality of life. The main components of the human eye include the cornea, retina, pupil, optic nerve, iris, sclera and lens. Among these, the retina plays a crucial role in vision: it receives incoming light, processes it, and converts it into electrical impulses that travel through the optic nerve to the brain. Diabetes is one of the most common causes of retinal damage and vision problems, making early awareness and intervention extremely important.

Diabetes is a chronic illness that develops when the pancreas produces insufficient insulin or when the body is unable to use the insulin it produces. Insulin is the hormone responsible for regulating blood sugar levels.

Without proper regulation, blood glucose rises—a condition known as hyperglycemia—which, if untreated, gradually damages various body systems, including blood vessels and nerves. In India, approximately 2.6 crore adults above the age of 18 have pre-diabetes, placing them at high risk of developing diabetes in the future.

An estimated 7.8 crore Indian adults are already living with type-2 diabetes. Despite its severity, more than half of those affected remain unaware of their condition. Diabetes significantly increases the risk of heart attacks and strokes—by nearly two to three times in adults.

Reduced blood circulation along with neuropathy (nerve damage) in the feet further increases the risk of infections, foot ulcers, and in severe cases, amputation. Diabetic retinopathy, caused by long-term damage to the small blood vessels in the retina, remains one of the leading causes of blindness. Globally, the number of people with diabetes is projected to rise from 1.72 crore in 2000 to 3.67 crore by 2030. At the time of diagnosis, up to 21% of patients with type-2 diabetes already show signs of retinopathy, and most eventually develop some degree of retinal damage. Currently, strict blood sugar control and routine check-ups are the primary methods of managing the condition. Retinal imaging plays a crucial role in diagnosing vision-related complications such as glaucoma, cataracts, Diabetic Macular Edema (DME), and Diabetic Retinopathy (DR). Annual eye examinations or regular screenings are strongly recommended for all diabetic individuals to detect abnormal blood vessel growth, retinal swelling and other early signs of damage.

1.2 THE ANATOMY OF EYE

Humans' visual system is composed of the optic nerves and their brain connections, the eyes and their supporting components [5]. The eye is a specialized photoreceptive organ as shown in Figure 1.1. The retina's rod and cone cells are modified as a consequence of the retina's processing of the light energy present in the surrounding environment. Changes in photo signals are translated by nerve function into information that the brain will consciously perceive as vision. The principal structures of the eye are the tunics (layers) that comprise the nearly spherical eyeball (typically 20 mm in diameter). The middle or vascular tunic is made up of ciliary body, choroid and iris, the retina is part of nerve tunic and cornea & sclera make up the fibrous tunic.

Human eye's vitreous cavity is filled with vitreous fluid. The outer covering of eyeball is called sclera and it is opaque, white, and tough. Its primary function is to secure the eye, maintain its shape and provide a point of attachment for the muscles that move the eye. The cornea is a transparent structure that conducts coarse focusing necessary for the vision and allows the light to pass through it and it is located in front of the sclera. Most of the blood arteries in eye are found in vascular tunic and choroid supplies 90% of the ocular blood flow. At the front of the eye, the ciliary bodies support the lens, the fine focusing element of the vision system, while the iris provides the variable aperture (pupil) required to adjust the quantity of light falling on the retina. The vitreous humor's function is to keep the intraocular pressure of the eye at the proper level in order to maintain the lens and retina's position.

Increased intraocular pressure is a symptom of the sight-threatening disease glaucoma, which needs to be treated very away. The whole refractive capacity of the eye is enhanced by the transparent, gelatinous fluid known as vitreous humor.

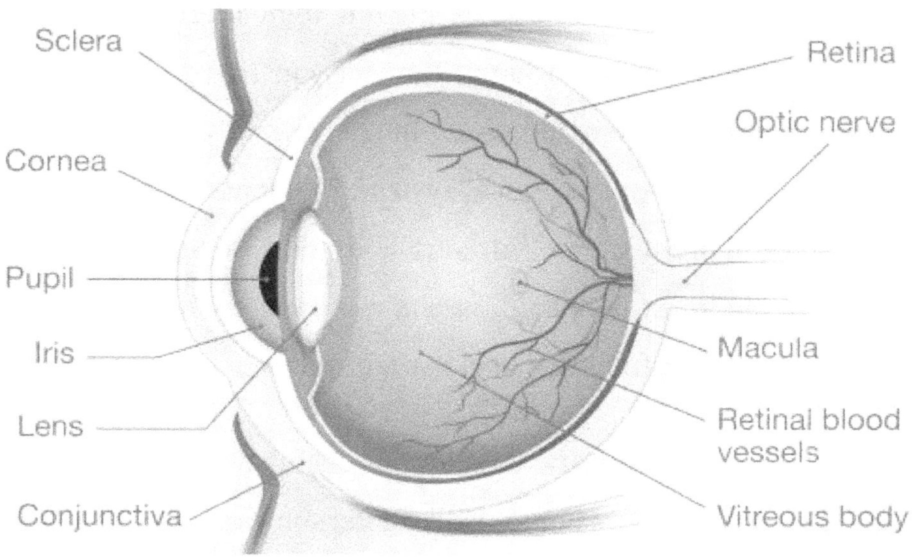

Figure 1.1 Anatomy structure of eye

1.3 EYE BALL

The diameter and volume of the eye are roughly 2.5 centimeters and 6.5 milliliters. Inside the eyeball are two spheres; the cornea has a greater curvature than the sclera, which has a large posterior sphere. Three tissue layers comprise the Eyeball, Lens and Iris. The outward layer of eye consists a rough, opaque sclera and transparent cornea, the latter allows light to enter the eye. Cornea is the first optical component encountered by light and forms one-sixth of the globe's circumference with a radius of 7.8mm. It is a transparent vascular structure made up of connective tissue matrix on the exterior and a solitary layer on the interior. The frontal chamber is enclosed by cornea and lens at the back. The clear fluid that fills the eye is called aqueous humor. It is a watery fluid that maintains intraocular pressure and nourishes the cornea and lens. The iris is a thin, contractile, circular, colored disk that normalizes the flow of light and functions similarly to the shutter in a camera. The diaphragm, also known as the pupil, dilates in dim light (eight millimeters) and constricts in intense light (one millimeter). In Figure 1.2, the Lens is a highly organized system composed of specialized cells (lens fibers) that is a key component of the optical system. The lens accommodates within its capsule, in front of the vitreous body and behind the cornea. It is typically a biconvex, ellipsoid, vascular structure with a different radius of curvature on the front and back surfaces.

The largest cavity, the vitreous chamber, is located between the retina and lens. Vitreous humor is like a gel substance that keeps the retina firmly against choroid, providing an even surface for the retina to receive a distinct image. The vitreous body differs from the aqueous humor in that it is not continuously replenished. The vitreous body contains phagocytes that clear the area of detritus, allowing for clear vision. The third layer that makes up the eyeball is the retina, which is the innermost and occupies approximately 1250 mm^2 of the ocular's surface area. This layer is the image plane of the optical system, which converts information from the image of the external environment into neural impulses for transmission to the brain for decoding and analysis.

The choroid is a highly vascularized middle layer of eyeball that lies posterior to retina and covers the majority of sclera's inner surface. Several blood vessels that supplies the posterior surface of retina, are connected to ciliary arteries that penetrate sclera in a ring surrounding the optic nerve. Choroid comprises melanocytes that generate the pigment melanin, which absorbs light and prevents it from reflecting and scattering inside the eyeball. Sclera is the impenetrable and white sclera. The sclera is the outer membrane of eyeball that encompasses the whole eyeball, excluding the cornea. It consists of dense connective tissue composed of collagen filaments and fibroblasts, which connects the muscles responsible for eye movement. It also maintains the eyeball's functional shape and stiffens it to secure its interior.

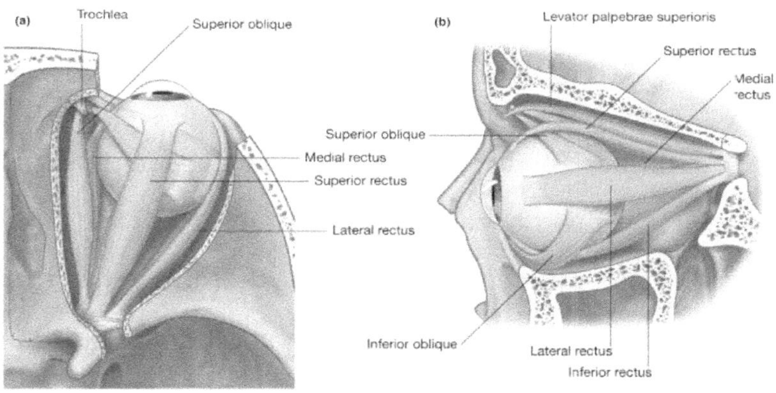

Figure 1.2 Anatomy structure of eyeball

1.4 RETINA

Retina is located between the choroid and the transparent central nucleus. A translucent gel with a concentrated formation differs in the crystal; as it approaches the retina, its central liquid phase gradually transforms into a fibrous system. Extending from the tesseract structure of systemic cells that supports pulmonary and neuro-sensory elements of retina, this is confined to a specific aspect of retinal blood vessels. RPE or retinal pigment epithelium, is the posterior corneal layer that extends outward from the center of eyeball. It is one of the corneal circulation disorders that have disrupted the eye's metabolism. In early DR lesions or moderate to moderate cases, the corneal interior is primarily located between building cells and crusted cells, along with the exterior of RPE.

The retina is a layered structure that is sensitive to light. Two-thirds of the interior portion of ocular globe is covered by the retina. Using a fundus ophthalmoscope, a clear image of several essential retinal structures, including blood vessels, optic nerve and macula can be observed.

1.5 DIABETIC RETINOPATHY IN RETINA

An injury to the retina's tiny blood vessels can occur when glucose levels in blood become too high for an extended period of time. Retinal membrane: inner layer of each eye. To allow the brain to perceive the outside world, the retina detects light and translates it into messages. One disorder brought on by injury to the retinal blood vessels is DR. Middle-aged people in industrialized countries who have diabetes often have diabetic retinopathy, a chronic illness that causes visual loss.

Diabetic retinopathy appears as tiny changes in the capillaries that supply the retina. Retinal micro infarcts lead to blood vessel blockage as retinopathy progresses as shown in Figure 1.3. Soft exudates are what are known as these little infarcts. The primary reason of blindness in many individuals is diabetic retinopathy, a medical disorder that arises from diabetes. Since dot hemorrhages are the initial indication of the ailment, identifying sick tissues is a necessary step in the diagnostic method. Often occurring causes of dot hemorrhages include diabetes, Ocular ischemia syndrome, sickle cell retinopathy, juxta foveal telangiectasia and retinal vein occlusions.

Diabetic retinopathy may be labeled into two main types: Proliferative Diabetic Retinopathy (PDR) and Non-Proliferative Diabetic Retinopathy (NPDR). Micro aneurysms, retinal hemorrhages, hard exudates and macular edema are related with NDR [6]. Both the retina and the vitreous may get scarred in PDR that follows due to new blood vessel development in the retina. Optical coherence tomography, retinal photography, fluorescence angiography and ophthalmoscopy are clinical techniques used to diagnose diabetic retina.

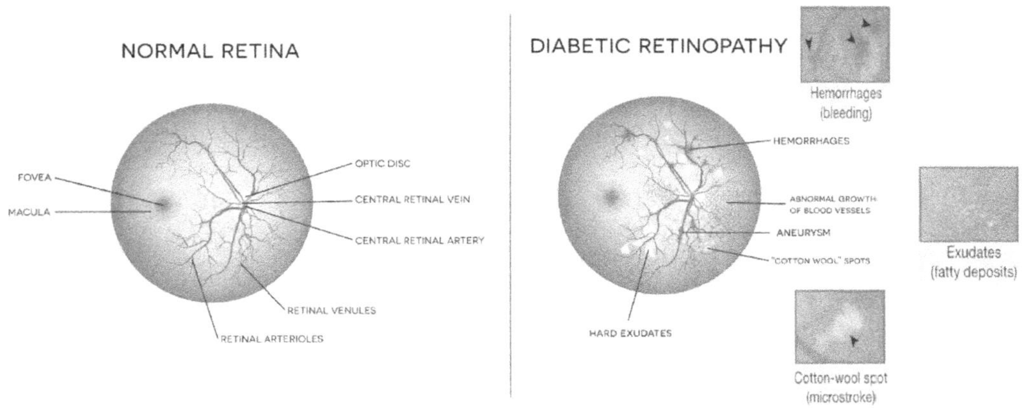

Figure 1.3 Normal retina and affected Diabetic Retinopathy [7]

1.6 TYPES OF RETINOPATHY

Diabetes-related retinal disease called "retinopathy" leads the retina's blood vessels to narrow. Two forms of retinopathy associated with diabetes:

1.6.1 Microaneurysms (MA)

Tiny, red, microscopic lumps protruding from the retina are called microaneurysms (MA). MAs are always visible in the color fundus picture as a tiny, spherical, dark red speck. The MAs have a spherical form, a diameter of 10 to 100 μm and a color that is comparable to blood vessels. The earliest discernible alteration in DR is these focal dilatations. MAs begin with thin walls, which later enlarge as a result of erythrocytes and fibrin building up inside the aneurysm. Figure 1.4 depicts the Microaneurysms appearance.

1.6.2 Hemorrhages (HMAS)

Damages to retinal tissue of the eye are identified as hemorrhages (HMAs). When microaneurysm capillaries thin out, they burst and release fluid, which results in hemorrhages. Hemorrhages are asymmetrical in shape and show as a dark crimson patch. Figure 1.4(a) depicts the hemorrhage structure.

Types of Hemorrhages:

- Dot hemorrhages
- Vitreous hemorrhages

Bright red dots represent dot hemorrhages that resemble MA, Deep Hemorrhages are shaped like circles or ovals. Blot hemorrhages are mainly located in the mid retinal area and look greater in size. Vitreous hemorrhage, often triggered by vascular perforation, can cause fresh blood particles and floaters, often resulting in diffuse clouding and inferiorly settled blood, especially in cases of proliferative diabetic retinopathy (Figure 1.4 b).

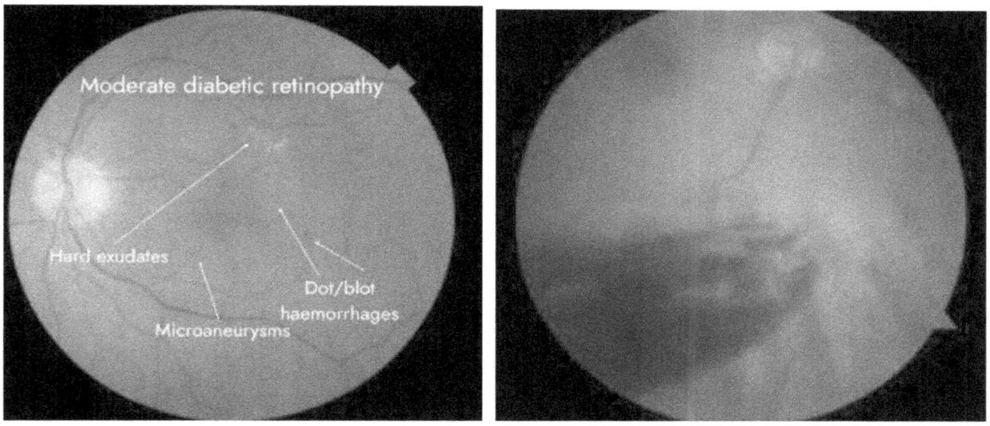

Figure 1.4 (a) The dot/blot hemorrhage (b) Vitreous hemorrhage

An internal bleeding disorder known as a vitreous hemorrhage affects vitreous humor, a translucent substance which fills the eye like gel between the retina and lens. Retinal tears, diabetic retinopathy, or age-related macular degeneration are few examples of underlying conditions that typically cause this disorder. Floaters, or dark patches or specks in vision and visual abnormalities can all be brought on by a vitreous hemorrhage. Diagnosing the source of the bleeding and maintaining or restoring eyesight require immediate examination and treatment by an ophthalmologist.

1.6.3 Symptoms of a Retinal Hemorrhage

Due to the importance of the retina to vision, diabetes, injuries and minor bleeding can cause vision problems such as blurred vision, blind patches and the perception of lines and streaks. Both eyeballs are susceptible. A vitreous hemorrhage occurs when blood escapes into the vitreous humor. Although a minor retinal hemorrhage may have few or no symptoms, a significant retinal hemorrhage can have the following symptoms:

- Floaters in the visual field.
- Observing cobwebs, lines, or trails.
- Vision with a hazy or distorted quality.
- Vision with a reddish hue.
- Vision impairment in the morning.

1.6.4 Exudates

In fundus imaging, exudates show up as bright, uneven patterns. In Figure 1.5, the appearance of exudates is displayed. These are the lipid and protein deposits that are discovered to seep from the abnormal retinal BV. Exudates come in two varieties: Soft Exudates (SE) and Hard Exudates (HE). Blood vessel protein deposits might be white, light white, or a combination of pale white and yellow exudates. HE is the term for glossy, yellow lipid and proteins are deposited in retina. They are buried far beneath the layers of the retina. Over time, lipid deposits build up, swell and leak, creating a circulatory pattern in the nearby capillaries [8].

1.6.5 Cotton wool patches

Soft exudates, also known as cotton wool patches, are cloud-like lesions that appear yellowish-white or grayish-white in color. Figure 1.5 depicts the structure of spots made of cotton wool. They become visible because of damage to the retina's nerve fibers. If Fovea is impacted, this could result in visual impairment. Cotton wool spots may show either alone or in combination with other spots [9].

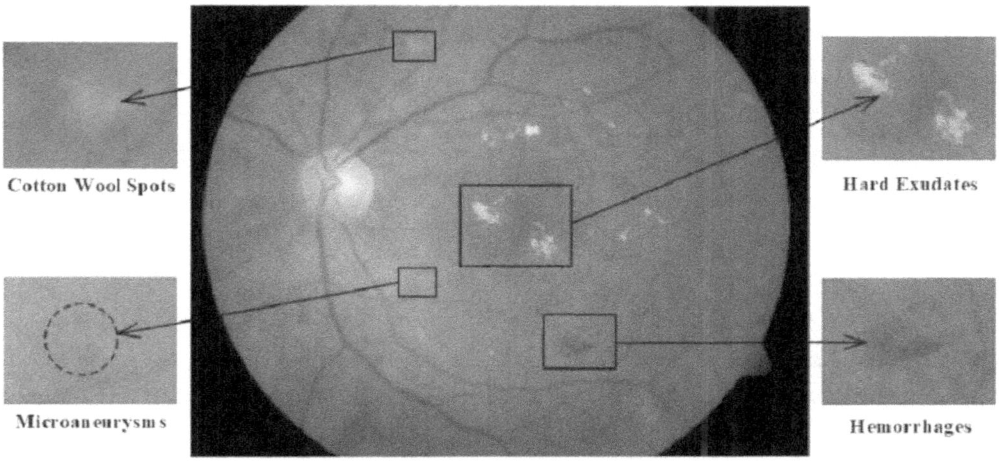

Figure 1.5 Different lesions of DR

The fundus images at each stage of DR are depicted in Figure 1.6. NPDR refers to the second, third and fourth phases, while PDR is the last stage.

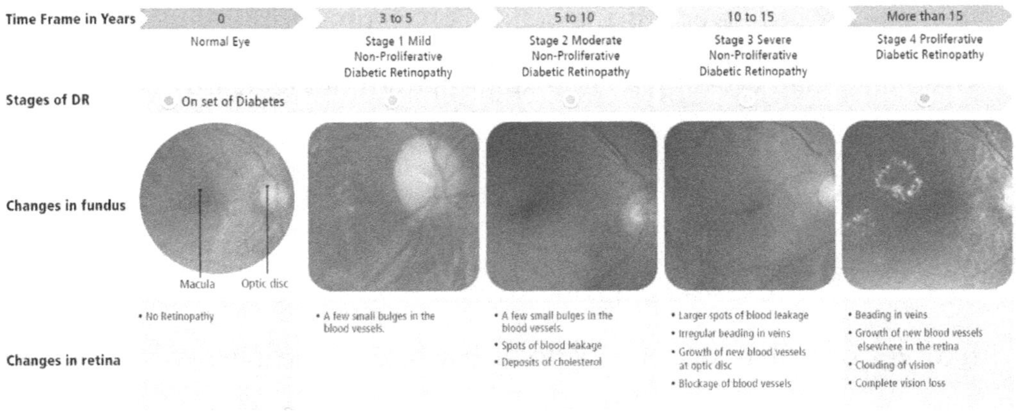

Figure 1.6 Stages of DR in fundus image

Table 1.1 provides details on various lesions, highlighting their distinct features and mechanisms.

Table 1.1 DR Lesions [10]

S. No.	DR lesions	Unique Features of Ophthalmoscopy	Mechanism
1	Micro-aneurysms	On retinal blood vessels, these tiny saccular structures appear as red spots.	Originates from the capillary wall's out-pouching.
2	Hemorrhages	Both dot and blot hemorrhages are possible.	Formed by freshly formed blood vessels that seep into the transparent, jelly-like material that occupies the eye's center.
3	Hard Exudate	Appears as tiny, sharply-bordered white or yellowish deposits.	Caused by deposits of blood lipids, such as cholesterol, seeping into the retina through pre-capillary capillaries
4	Cotton Wool Spot	On the retina, fluffy gray-white patches are typically found close to the optic disc.	As a result of nerve fiber injury

1.7 HEMORRHAGES IN RETINA

A condition known as Retinal Hemorrhage (RH) causes bleeding in many retinal layers located in the rear of the eye. RH can be caused by hypertension or by a common problem called central retinal vein occlusion. Retinal Hemorrhages are an essential ophthalmic diagnostic indicator of a systemic RH is a disorder in which there is multilayered bleeding in the retinal tissue of the posterior wall of the eye. RH can be brought on by hypertension or the prevalent disease known as central retinal vein occlusion. One crucial ocular diagnostic marker of a systemic vascular disease is retinal hemorrhages. The mildest dot-and-blot hemorrhage to the most serious subhyaloid hemorrhage can be found among them. The location, extent and distribution of the hemorrhages can reveal underlying systemic conditions, such as trauma, hypoxia, dyscrasias, hematologic diseases, vascular diseases and infections. Most hemorrhages have an underlying cause that requires careful, meticulous study to identify. Therapy comprises of intraocular care to reduce the ischemia and neovascularization scream caused by the hemorrhage, as well as surveillance and treatment of the underlying cause.

Retinal hemorrhage is an eye condition marked by bleeding in the retina. In the retina, cones and rods are two types of photoreceptor cells, converts light energy into nerve electrical signals, processing by brain to produce visual images as depicted in Figure 1.7.

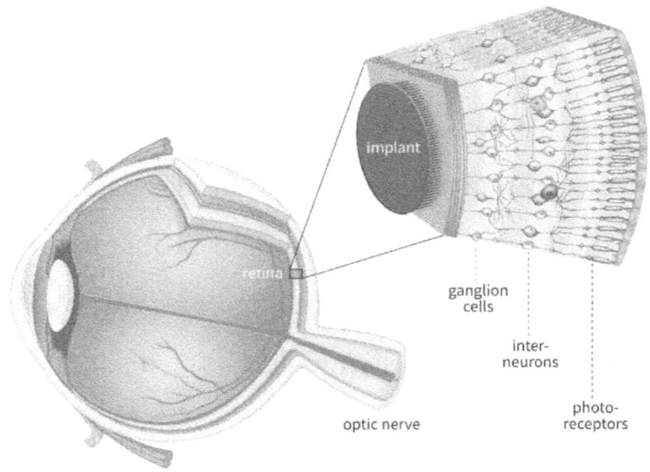

Figure 1.7 Photoreceptor- Rods and Cones

Diabetes may cause damage to the body's blood vessels. When sugar clogs a tiny blood arteries supplying your retina Figure 1.8 (a), it can lead to bleeding or fluid leakage Figure 1.8 (b), which is the first step toward damage to your eyes. To compensate these clogged blood vessels, the eyes produces a new and less functioning's blood vessels.

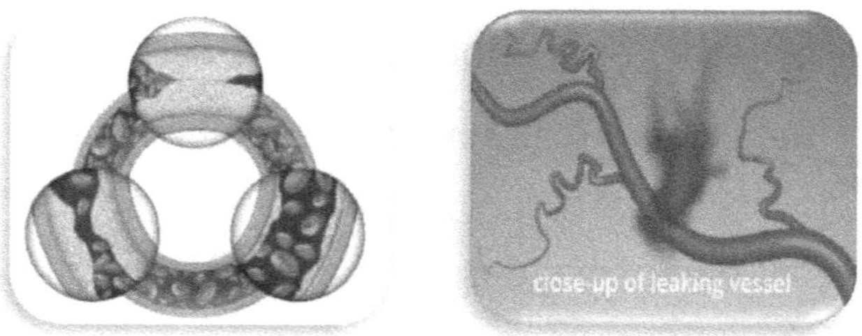

Figure 1.8 a) Sugar clogs b) Blood leakage

The brain creates fresh and weaker blood vessels in reaction to pressure that builds up the network of blood vessels because of insufficient oxygen and elevated blood sugar levels. The brain makes these new, weaker blood vessels because the existing blood vessels are unable to send signals to the brain. Because of this, the capillaries in the retina become fragile and cause hemorrhages that resemble flames, dots, or blots to occur. Although retinal fires are caused by the rupture of retinal nerve fibers, dots are frequently linked to diabetic retinopathy. They look as distinct-edged objects or things with uneven shapes on the retina.

RH is a condition characterized by bleeding in different retinal tissue layers on the eye's posterior side. Hypertension or blockage of the central retinal vein, a common condition, can lead to RH. Additionally, the disease is common among child victims of cerebral trauma caused by abuse. Along with cerebral hemorrhage and edema, RH is one of the essential criteria in the triad of pathological symptoms of shaken infant syndrome. It is believed to be the outcome of abusive shaking's recurrent acceleration and deceleration pressures. The vitreous humor, a fluid-filled chamber that occupies most of the eye and rests next to the retina, has been suggested as the site of the damage process, wherein inertial forces cause traction.

Today, most people understand that any process that increases the brain's intracranial pressure (ICP) can cause retinal hemorrhages. Since the optic nerve and retinal vasculature are enclosed within the eye, they represent the only superficially visible portion of the Central Nervous System (CNS), is capable of reflecting changes in intracranial pressure. Elevated back pressure in the retinal capillaries can result from increases in arterial pressure, for the reason arterial pressure is greater than venous pressure and it can obstruct blood flow through the central retinal vein. There may be retinal hemorrhages as a result of the capillaries rupturing from the increased pressure. Bilateral RH are prevalent when excessive ICP, or intracranial pressure, is primary reason for the amount of bleeding usually corresponds with the ICP level.

The degree of retinal hemorrhages associated with abusive head trauma in infants has been indicated to be different from other forms of trauma. With many retinal and sub retinal layers affected and spreading all the way to the anterior border of the retina, ora serrata, they are frequently more comprehensive.

Additionally, the duration of elevated ICP is a factor in determining the severity of RH. Ophthalmologic tests are usually performed in situations of suspected abusive head trauma in babies; since RH are not life-threatening, the examination can wait until all immediate assessments and treatments are finished. The frequency and intensity of RHs may rise throughout this period until ICP is reduced by time, therapy, or mortality.

The correlation between RH and abusive head trauma is not limited to this particular cause of child death. Compared to instances requiring cerebral edema and advanced life support, those involving RH and Optic Nerve Sheath Hemorrhage (ONSH) were more common. According to recent research, a 7-month-old neonates who had a recorded brief fall had bilateral RH and ONSH. Non-pediatric populations are also susceptible to RH, especially those who are engaged in activities that involve substantial internal and external pressure changes, such weightlifting and deep-sea diving. The majority of the time, retinal hemorrhages and optic nerve sheath hemorrhages are sensitive indications of abusive head trauma, but they are not very specific since they can also occur in circumstances in which there is no deliberate harm.

Hemorrhages in the retina are indicative of systemic vascular disease in the eyes. The least severe sub-hyaloids hemorrhage is accompanied by the mildest dot and blot hemorrhage. The distribution, location and size of retinal hemorrhages can reveal systemic problems that are not immediately apparent, such as hematologic disorders, vascular diseases, dyscrasias, infections, hypoxia and trauma. To identify the underlying cause of most hemorrhages, a comprehensive systemic examination is necessary. Treatment includes observation, addressing the primary reason and key factors in managing intraocular conditions are to reduce the risk of lack of blood supply (ischemia) and new blood vessel formation (neovascularization) caused by hemorrhages.

The neuron that is sensitive to light is located in the rear of the eye is called retina. RH is eye disorder characterized by bleeding within the retina. In infant and early children, RH is strongly linked to child maltreatment and frequently causes the infants to become permanently blind. Elderly children and adults may experience retinal hemorrhage due to a variety of medical disorders, such as hypertension, diabetes, anemia, leukemia and retinal vein occlusion. All of the body's blood vessels are damaged by diabetes. When sugar clogs the tiny blood arteries supplying your retina, it can lead to bleeding or fluid leakage, which is the first step towards damage to your eyes. In the eyes, ineffective blood vessels grow to replace the blocked ones.

Retinal hemorrhages occur in 15% of very sick infants who have never experienced trauma or maltreatment. Significant coagulopathy, unintentional brain damage and systemic infection are associated with the majority of mild cases, which affect children under the age of two. Birth-related retinal hemorrhages occur in 25% of neonates delivered naturally and 40% to 50% of infants delivered using instrumentation. RH affect 30% of infants who are physically mistreated and most of them are younger than six months. Because most systemic illnesses are more common in persons over 40, this age group is also the most common for RH.

The brain creates new, weaker blood vessels in response to the pressure that builds up within the blood vessel network as a result of oxygen deprivation and high blood glucose levels. The brain creates new, weaker blood vessels that are unable to effectively transmit signals to it. Capillaries are so fragile, this causes flame and dot or blot shaped hemorrhages in the retina. Dots are commonly linked to diabetic retinopathy, while retinal flame hemorrhages arise from the rupture of retinal nerve fibers. On the retina, these appear as irregularly shaped or distinctly edged lesions.

1.8 ETIOLOGY

Retinal hemorrhages may be present in the following conditions, varying with the severity of the disease:

1. Ocular illnesses include optic disc hemorrhages, Age-Related Macular Degeneration (ARMD), juxta foveal telangiectasia and Polypoidal Choroidal Vasculopathy (PCV).

2. Dot hemorrhages: Diabetic retinopathy is characterized by dot lesions and hemorrhages seen in the vitreous. Throughout the posterior pole, bilateral and widely scattered.

3. Hypertensive retinopathy: Rarely observed are preretinal hemorrhages and diffuse flame-shaped hemorrhages in hypertensive retinopathy.

4. Occlusions of the retinal veins: all quadrants experience diffuse intraretinal hemorrhages in cases of central retinal vein occlusions; with regard to branch retinal vein occlusions the distribution is sectoral.

5. Trauma: Bilateral or unilateral multi-layered hemorrhages are possible, depending on the kind of damage. Retinal hemorrhages are a hallmark of both Valsalva retinopathy and Terson syndrome. Children and infants with shaken newborn syndrome exhibit bilateral diffuse multi-layered hemorrhages. The primary cause of neonatal retinal hemorrhages is birth trauma.

6. Anemia: The following are signs of anemia: subhyaloid hemorrhages, vitreous hemorrhages, multi-layered hemorrhages and Roth spots. They are observed to be bilaterally dispersed.

7. Leukemia: The symptoms of leukemia include cotton wool spots, hemorrhages like flame shaped, vitreous, intraretinal, Roth spots and preretinal. Neovascularization of sea-fans is a typical observation. Bilaterally observed and widely dispersed.

8. Acute bacterial endocarditis: Cotton wool spots, Roth spots, intraretinal or flame shaped hemorrhages close to the papillary

edge and preretinal or vitreous hemorrhages are its defining features. They are visible on both sides.

9. Sickle cell anemia: The SC induce black sunburst chorioretinal ischemia scarring, intraretinal salmon patch hemorrhages, sea fan revascularization, this can result in vitreous hemorrhage and retinopathy, which are observable from both perspectives.

10. Ocular ischemia syndromes: retinal neovascularization, mid-peripheral intraretinal hemorrhages.

11. Preeclampsia: The condition is characterized by serous retinal detachment, Elschnig patches and intraretinal hemorrhages. They are discernible in differing degrees on both sides.

12. Intraretinal hemorrhage and vascular occlusions are observed in both eyes in severe stages of supportive tissue illnesses, such as lupus.

13. High altitude retinopathy: Bilateral high altitude retinopathy commonly manifests as Roth spots, vitreous hemorrhages and multi-layered hemorrhages.

1.9 SYMPTOMS OF A RETINAL HAEMORRHAGE

Due to the importance of the retina to vision, diabetes, injuries, and minor bleeding can cause vision problems such as blurred vision, blind patches and the perception of lines and streaks. Both eyeballs are susceptible. A vitreous hemorrhage occurs when blood escapes into the vitreous humor (colorless gel like substance located between the retina and lens). Although a minor retinal hemorrhage may have few or no symptoms, a significant retinal hemorrhage can have the following symptoms:

- Floaters in the visual field.
- Observing cobwebs, lines, or trails.
- Vision with a hazy or distorted quality.
- Vision with a reddish hue.
- Vision impairment in the morning.

1.10 EARLY DETECTION OF RETINAL HAEMORRHAGES

In United States and European Union, diabetic dot hemorrhages causes a blindness in adult age of working individuals. Patients with diabetic retinal issues can avoid blindness and vision loss by using screening to diagnose the condition early and get the correct therapy. The amount of people living with diabetes in US will rise in each age group, the average age will rise, and there will soon be a scarcity of skilled eye care professionals, according to forecasts for the United States during the next ten years. This "perfect storm" of healthcare trends will challenge the public health system's ability to manage both patients with retinal hemorrhages and those with diabetes who are at risk for these complications. If the aforementioned scenario occurs, it’s necessary to screen a large number of diabetics for retinal DH, limit access to eye care, or implement both measures.

Using digital photography and skilled picture interpretation, a few European countries have successfully launched early detection programs for diabetic retinal hemorrhages. In 2007–2008, 1.7 million diabetics in the United Kingdom were screened for diabetic retinal hemorrhages. Since 2001, more than 30,000 persons with diabetes have been screened in the Netherlands through the Eye Check early detection program. In 2008, the Department of Veterans Affairs (VA) launched a successful photo screening program at VA medical centers, resulting in the screening of 120,883 patients.

To enhance the early detection of retinal dot hemorrhages, numerous computer image analysis methods employing image processing and ML have been developed in the past decade to analyze digital retinal images. In a group with a low prevalence of diabetic retinal dot hemorrhages, which would be typical of screening populations, only a small number of these approaches have been studied on a substantial scale.

After some initial success, we have been coming up with fresh methods in order to increase algorithms' efficiency. In recent years, we have only obtained modest performance enhancements by adding complexity to the algorithms. We believe that small improvements in performance, despite being meaningful, will become more challenging to quantify due to known intra and inter observer variability of human readers, against whom these algorithms are compared. The implementation of a global online diabetic retinal dot hemorrhages detection algorithm is the method we chose to maximize performance.

The sensitivity and specificity of detecting diabetic retinal dot hemorrhages must be assessed to evaluate whether this type of algorithms are close to or exceed those values. As there is no singular sensitivity and specificity, this issue cannot be clearly answered because different readers will experience sensitivity and specificity differently depending on their education, experience and other circumstances.

The algorithms' performance can be compared to that of single reader or a small group of readers and we can evaluate their development, whether or not we can expect further performance improvements. According to our theory, algorithms for detecting diabetic retinal dot hemorrhages are mature, or close to the performance threshold that can be assessed and they can detect these lesions with sensitivity and specificity similar to the results of a single human expert.

We believe early detection of diabetic retinal DH to be the largest burden, therefore, the automated algorithms presented here are intended to suggest referring any patient with any type of condition of diabetic retinal DH to an ophthalmologist. However, they might be altered to detect patients with severe non-proliferative DR, widespread CSME, or proliferative DR, which would diagnosis vision-threatening diabetic retinopathy. However, current early detection programs-not those that have just been started-underrepresent this category.

We have previously designed and tested systems that recognize cotton-wool spots and exudates, but in order to guarantee a more precise comparison, the algorithms were limited to recognizing only red lesions (microaneurysms and small hemorrhages). As a result, the automated algorithms are enhanced to propose ophthalmologist referral for patients with any type of diabetic retinal hemorrhages.

1.11 CHALLENGES IN AI OPHTHALMOLOGY

Artificial Intelligence has ability to enhance the patients by accessing ophthalmic diagnosis and screening, assist in referral triage, advance treatment when necessary and monitor patient outcomes [11]. Nevertheless, there are real-world obstacles to widespread clinical applications of AI in ophthalmology, such as

1. The accessibility of a verified AI solution fit to real-world implementation using DL methods with clinically appropriate demonstration and the capacity to obtain images of various excellence from widely used equipment in a normal healthcare setting.

2. Resolving problems with the diverse patient group, acquisition guidelines and image quality.

3. Addressing the moral and legal fallout from using AI in healthcare.

4. Creating a uniform reporting format and agreed-upon standards for diagnosis, referral, and triage

5. Negotiating technological obstacles and ambiguities.

1.12 AI IN OPHTHALMOLOGY

The phrase Artificial Intelligence (AI) refers to the overall task by a computer with minimal human intervention. In other words, the purpose of artificial intelligence is to make computers replicate our thought processes and increase our productivity in today's rapidly evolving world. It has become one of the most influential revolutions in information technology. As far as we can tell, theoretical research and its applications have advanced significantly. AI is widely accepted as the origin of numerous robots in various disciplines, particularly bioinformatics. There have been instances of successful robot-assisted surgery when combined with medicine. It makes physicians' labor more precise and efficient. Currently, image-based AI-assisted medical surveillance and diagnosis are emerging. As we all know, melanoma, a form of skin cancer, could be diagnosed using an algorithm based on macro images captured by a standard camera. Using this AI technology relies heavily on machine learning, which is exemplified by mathematical algorithms and models derived from vast amounts of experience input.

The clinical application of ML in AI was first demonstrated in 1976 with the CASNET-based glaucoma consulting software. Ophthalmology, a medical specialty that heavily depends on imaging and data, may hold the greatest potential for AI implementation. DL algorithms tailored for ophthalmology are based on the concept of disease-based learning. In this approach, a physician labels specific disease features on an image, allowing the computer to identify and learn from them. The machine's output is then validated by comparing it to disease signs identifiable by experienced hominid observers. Interestingly, Google Intelligence DL system, using a method known as image grounded learning, independently obtained the capacity to accurately recognize a features of DR in an anonymized images. The most capable AI tools presently available for retinal diseases focus on DR, Retinopathy of Prematurity (ROP) and Age-Related Macular

Degeneration (AMD). AI is also significant in areas beyond oculoplastic surgery, including anterior segment conditions like keratoconus, cataracts and glaucoma. This covers topics such as AI-based retinal screening, ultrasound technology and glaucoma applications.

1.13 AI IN OPHTHALMOLOGY RESEARCH

Conventional feature based ML approaches were the foundation of AI applications in ophthalmology. These ML techniques needed ophthalmologists with specialized training to identify specific clinical traits and severities in images to develop AI systems. This process is called "supervised learning." Artificial intelligence systems were trained on these annotated images to categorize an images according to recognition of these feature descriptors. Deployment Learning-(DL) is a novel artificial intelligence approach that is trained without requiring expert-labelled feature labels; it functions through "unsupervised learning". With complete image labels provided by experts based on clinical diagnosis or severity, DL allows the AI to "self-learn" the predicted features.

Recent studies have demonstrated the clinical acceptability of various DL algorithms for categorizing Color Fundus Photography (CFP) data from ophthalmic imaging for a change of ocular ailments, including dry eye syndrome. Optical Coherence Tomography (OCT) scan classification is among the successful applications. Because OCT imaging provides granular 3-dimensional information rather than 2-dimensional information, it could increase the efficacy of the screening methods that are based on CFP. Fortunately, retinal features associated with the severity and clinical results have been determined for major eye disorders like DR, AMD and glaucoma, permitting the training of DL for classification of ophthalmic images. A new study highlights the progress made in developing DL systems for a diversity of applications, encompassing the classification of DR in OCT and CFPs images. The DL that identify glaucoma in ocular imaging and classify AMD in CFPs that predict the reports of AMD development utilizing OCTs and some of them have been demonstrated in actual datasets obtained from screening settings such as glaucoma clinics and tele-ophthalmology.

1.14 METHODS TO PROCESS THE IMAGES

Prior to beginning image processing, it is essential to understand the elements of the image. Pixel count that make up an image's height and width. For example, 200000 total pixels are included in an image with the following dimensions: width x height = 500 x 400. Each pixel in the image has a certain tone, opacity, or hue assigned to it. One of the following usually serves as a representation of it: Gray scale: A pixel's value falls between 0 and 255, with 0 denoting complete darkness and 255 denoting complete whiteness. The three values that make up an RGB pixel range from 0 to 255, which represents red, green and blue [12]. The alpha field that is added to RGBA represents the opacity of the image and is an extension of RGB. To process an image, every pixel needs to go through a set of steps. The image processor handles the initial set of actions on the image pixel by pixel. It will start the following operation as soon as this is finished and so on. Any image pixel can be used to determine the operation's output value.

What is involved in Image processing technique?

Image processing includes transforming converting images into a digital file and executing certain operations on it to extract useful images. An image processing system uses predefined signal processing algorithms to handle all images as two dimensional signals.

1.15 IMAGE PROCESSING TYPES

Image processing is divided into five main categories:

1. Visualization - Identify invisible objects in an image identify or distinguish pixels in an image.

2. Image sharpening and restoration - Develop an enhanced image that improves upon source image.

3. Pattern recognition - Analyze the patterns that surrounds the object within the image.

4. Retrieval - A huge collection of digital images which closely resembles with originals that may be explored and viewed.

1.16 ESSENTIAL IMAGE PROCESSING METHODS

Image capture:

The primary stage of any image processing process is image capture, as features and quality of image will have an immediate effect on all other processing procedures. Getting the image from a source usually a piece of hardware is the initial step in the procedure, which is also referred to preprocessing.

Contrast improvement:

Finding and highlighting hidden aspects in an image is the process of image enhancement, or contrast enhancement. This may need altering the brightness, contrast and other settings.

Image Retouching:

To improve an image look is to do image restoration. Unlike image enhancement, however, image restoration employs specific models that use mathematics or statistics.

Using color to process images:

Digital color modeling techniques are used widely in color picture processing. This stage has become more significant as a result of how frequently digital images are used online.

Wavelets and Multiresolution Processing:

Wavelets are mathematical operations that allow for localized analysis by dissecting images into constituents at various sizes and locations. Applications like image compression, denoising and feature extraction benefit greatly from multiresolution processing, which use wavelets to represent data at several levels of detail.

Compression:

In image processing, compression minimizes duplication while maintaining crucial visual information, hence reducing the size of image files. Discrete Cosine Transform (DCT) and wavelet transform are two of the methods used by techniques like JPEG and PNG to accomplish compression. Reducing the amount of storage and transmission while maintaining image quality.

Morphological Operations:

The methods for processing images based on their structure include morphological operations. These techniques, which are most commonly used on binary pictures, probe and alter the pixel arrangement using a structural element. The two fundamental processes are dilation (growing object bounds) and erosion (shrinking object boundaries are used to eliminate noise, separate objects and improve structures within a picture. Morphological operations are commonly utilized in applications like edge detection, image segmentation and object recognition.

Image Segmentation:

In image processing technique, segmentation involves partitioning an image into relevant regions or segments, typically to segregate objects or features of interest. Numerous methods can be employed to complete this operation like thresholding, wherein the intensity values of the pixels are categorized, or edge based techniques that identify the borders between several areas. Segmentation is critical for applications like as object detection, image recognition and medical imaging, which require precise structural demarcation for analysis and interpretation.

Characteristics and Representation:

Every region that has been separated into segments of an image is then represented and defined in a way that can be processed further by a computer. Characteristics and regional attributes of a picture are the focus of representation. The process of description involves the extraction of quantitative data that sets one category of things apart from another [13-15].

1.17 IMAGE COMPARISON

Image comparison is a fundamental method in image processing. Comparing two images might sometimes be necessary to determine how similar or distinct they are from one another. To make choosing visualization and simulation parameters easier, images often need to be contrasted. In image analysis, estimating image similarity is a crucial problem. It is helpful to compare image similarity measures when assessing strategies for image matching, noise reduction, image coding and image restoration. This research covers tools and methods for comparing images. The color of pixels in an image with the same coordinates is contrasted by the comparison engine. Test complete considers two images to be same if each pixel in the images is the same color [16].

A. Methods

Pixel-by-pixel comparison:

Pixels with the same image coordinates are compared for color by the comparison engine. If every pixel in two images has the same color, Test Complete deems the images to be identical. There are several variables in the comparison engine. Every parameter allows bitmaps to be processed further, increasing the comparison's flexibility.

Pixel Tolerance

(In scripting approaches, known as Pixel Tolerance): Indicates the maximum number of dissimilar pixels that are permitted. Test complete views the images as being same, if the quantity of distinct pixels is the same as the pixel tolerance or less. For instance, two pixels separate the two bitmaps, if the Pixel Tolerance parameter is set to 2, Test Complete would classify these bitmaps as the same object.

Color Tolerance

(In scripting approaches, color tolerance): Defines the permissible color variation between two pixels in order for them to be regarded as identical. An integer number between 0 and 255 that indicates the maximum difference allowed for each of the three color components like red, green and blue pixels under comparison to represents color difference. If the difference between the brightness of the two pixels' respective color components does not go above a certain threshold, then two pixels are considered to be equal. The default value of Color Tolerance is 0, which means that only pixels that have the exact same color are regarded as identical. Pixels of all hues are treated equally when Color Tolerance is set to 255.

Comparison Mask:

Uses a mask - an image made up of black and white pixels - to define the regions of bitmaps that need to be compared. When the comparison engine employs a mask it processes the white pixels on the mask as relevant for comparison, while black pixels are ignored. Unlike the transparent parameter, there is no need to alter the original image; instead, a new image is created.

B. Image comparison utilizing the Hausdorff distance:

Each point in a model set that is close to a point in an image set is quantified by the Hausdorff distance and vice versa. As a result, the resemblance between two superimposed items can be determined using this distance. Effective methods for determining the Hausdorff distance between a binary image and a model at any feasible relative point are described.

The primary focus is on the scenario where the model is restricted to translation relative to the image, applying the methods to cases where motion is stationary. Unlike most other shape comparison techniques, the Hausdorff distance calculation does not establish a direct correspondence among the model and image. The procedure can accommodate minor positional errors, as arising from edge detectors and other feature extraction methods.

C. Distance based comparative functions for images:

Digital picture comparison continues to pique the interest of the computer vision community. A suitable comparison metric for non-binary pictures must be defined for many image processing applications. Assessing equivalency classes is essential for visual tasks like categorization and segmentation. In content-based picture retrieval systems, similarity metrics are also employed to establish pictorial indices and assess lossy compression algorithms. We offer multiple image distances based on low-level features and assess image similarity using a distance-based method. Three additional distance-based picture operations are available for digital image comparison. Because only digital images - not the scenes or objects they depict-are compared using low-level techniques, we are able to highlight the digital nature of the images. The experimental findings show that, in comparison to traditional intensity-based measures, merging global intensity and local structural aspects improves the sensitivity of the functions.

D. Techniques for detecting the changes in an image:

There is a general interest in finding areas of variance in many images taken at various times of same scene due to a wide range of diverse applications, including security, remote sensing, underwater sensing, medical diagnostics and therapy. Preprocessing techniques, prediction models, shading models, backdrop modeling, significance and hypothesis testing, and other relevant elements are only a few of the many processing stages and basic decision procedures that are thoroughly analyzed in the most recent methods for change detection.

E. Techniques for Preprocessing: Geometric Adjustments

- Radiometric/Intensity Modifications
- Intensity Standardization
- Homomorphic Filtration Lighting Modeling
- Transformations of Intensity that Are Linear
- Sudden Changes in Illumination
- Speckle Noise
- Predictive models
- Spatial models
- Temporal model

F. Comparison Based on Image Features:

An image feature in computer vision is a mathematical representation of the raw image. Comparing picture features is generally more accurate and efficient than comparing raw images. Three steps are involved in feature-based picture comparison: feature matching, feature description and feature detection.

1) The identification of picture features, such as corner points, is the goal of feature detection. 2) Determining the detected feature points is the second step in the picture comparison process.

The descriptor must to be distinct and unaffected by geometric, photometric and noise distortions. The histogram of the oriented local gradients surrounding the key point serves as the feature descriptor in the Scale Invariant Feature Transform (SIFT). Typically, a vector with 128 entries contains the histogram bins. 64 Haar wavelet replies typically make up the descriptor in SURF (Speeded up Robust Feature).

Feature matching is the third stage of picture comparison. Euclidean distance is the similarity metric used by both SIFT and SURF since all feature descriptor entries have equal magnitudes and can thus be appropriately adjusted.

G. Comparative statistics of images using Gibbs random fields:

Multivariate statistics often serve as the foundation for statistical methods that compare images by using images as observations. The spatial and dependency structures found in images are ignored by this method. Here, we employ an alternative method in which the quantity of observations is denoted by the number of pixels in the photographs. We also take dependency and spatial patterns into consideration by modeling images with Gibbs random fields that incorporate nearest neighbor interactions. The suggested method for comparing images aims to test for parameter equality between the aggregated images of each group by modeling the images using finite parameter Gibbs random fields.

We derive an easily calculable test statistic with a chi-square distribution as its limiting distribution. Applications for pattern recognition and handwritten signatures are presented.

1.18 A NOVEL ARCHITECTURE FOR FULLY AFFINE INVARIANT IMAGE COMPARISON

Images of a physical item taken by cameras at different angles will show smooth seeming deformations if the object's border is smooth or piecewise smooth. Affine transformations of the picture plane provide a good local approximation for these deformations. As a result, affine invariant image local feature computation has often been simplified to the recognition of solid objects. Such invariant qualities could be derived by normalization techniques, albeit there isn't a fully affine normalization technique at the moment. The only method that strictly addresses scale invariance is the SIFT methodology. SIFT can mimic zooming out and adjust for translation and rotation, making it invariant to four of the six parameters in an affine transform.

This novel introduces Affine-SIFT (ASIFT), by adjusting the two latitude and longitude angles-the remaining camera axis orientation parameters-from the SIFT technique, simulates every conceivable image perspective. The SIFT algorithm then handles the remaining four parameters. Mathematics will be used to demonstrate that the resulting procedure is entirely affine invariant.

Comparative Study of an Efficient Algorithm for Defect Identification in Gray-Level Digital Pictures Employing the ICA, Gabor and median filters. To obtain precise data regarding the pixel attributes, the feature extraction process is applied to every row in the image. The algorithm is compared to current methods, such the optimal Gabor filter method and Independent Component Analysis method (ICA). This simple and fast technique uses segmentation and feature extraction to find flaws in gray level digital images. Defects can be found by using detail matrices having median, maximum and minimum points. Optimized Gabor filters and Wavelet sub band can be used for texture flaw identification. Fabric flaws can be found with Gabor filters by applying Bernoulli's rule of combination.

Segmentation is used to find defects in the garment production system. A method called image removal is employed to find flaws in patterned textiles. To build the feature vector, the minimum, maximum and median values are computed for each image row. The high frequency components are removed by utilizing each row's median value. Next, defected points with abrupt changes in intensity from the preceding image element or from the median value are found using the low frequency component image and each row's median value.

Visual Evaluation for Image Comparison:

Image comparison methods that are well-established usually align images side by side. One major disadvantage of these approaches is their incapacity to grow. Other methods of comparing images use abstract factors like hue to encode differences between images. Thus, information about the underlying image information is lost. This is a revolutionary approach that allows the study of small differences and preserves contextual information while showing differences and similarities in big image sets. This approach uses cluster analysis techniques to identify local modifications and embed them in a hierarchy. Following this process, the outcomes are displayed in an interactive web application that lets users quickly explore the universe of differences and focus on particular traits.

1.19 THE N. LEAST SQUARES IMAGE MATCHING ALGORITHM

A great degree of matching precision has been achieved by the wide application and study of least squares image matching (LSM). Still, there are still certain problems with it. It needs to have a precise estimation of its starting value first. However, erroneous critical point placement may introduce biases into early values in real-world applications. There may be divergent answers if these biases are large enough. Matching biases are regarded as systematic errors if they are of the same size and direction.

Second, photographs with dead or stuck pixels could be the consequence of an imaging sensor breakdown. In the language of statistics, these are known as outliers. Due to the well-known vulnerability of least squares estimation to outliers, every one of these variations from the model as defined by LSM leads to an inability to match. In order to overcome these problems, a range of robust estimate techniques, including the RANSAC-based approach, the M, S and MM estimators, are used and contrasted in LSM experiments that include systematic errors and outliers. Furthermore, a criterion for evaluating ground truth-related to performance comparison of these robust estimators is suggested. Robust estimators offer greater resilience to these deviations compared to LSM. Among all the estimators, M and MM are the most effective.

1.20 RETINAL IMAGE INFORMATION BASE

The algorithms developed by researchers are tested and evaluated using databases of fundus images that are accessible to the public. These databases provide a common comparison platform. The internet provides access to numerous databases, including DRIVE, STARE, MESSIDOR, DIARETDB0, DIARETDB1, Kaggle, IDRiD, etc. These are some of the most frequently used databases employed in this study [17-18]:

1.20.1 Structured Analysis of Retina (STARE)

In the STARE database, used for blood vessel segmentation, 10 out of 380 images were found to be pathological. Among databases of its type, it is the most frequently used. A TopConTRC-50x fundus camera photographs the digitized images at 350 fields of vision. Digitization of the transparencies was done using 24 bits per color channel at a 600 x 700 pixel resolution. There are 31 healthy and 50 diseased images make up the STARE subgroup. These were used for the OD's localization by Hoover and GoldBaum. The National Institutes of Health supplied financing for Michael Goldbaum's STARE initiative, from the University of California in 1975. This project has been supported by more than thirty people with a variety of expertise, including engineering, scientific and medical.

The University of California, San Diego's Shiley Eye Center and the Veterans Administration Medical Centre in San Diego contributed images and clinical data for the database.

1.20.2 Standard Diabetic Retinopathy Database (DIARETDB)

Composed of DIARETDB-0 and DIARETDB-1, respectively. They are freely accessible to researchers used to assess the performance of an algorithm for the diagnosis of diabetic retinopathy. This publicly accessible database provides a benchmark for comparing the outcomes. The DIARETDB-0 database contains 20 standard retinal images and 110 pictures showing signs of pathology, including micro aneurysms, hemorrhages, hard exudates, cotton wools and revascularization. Color fundus images are available in DIARETDB1 database; No indications of diabetic retinopathy can be seen in five of these images, which are normal, conversely, the remaining 84 images clearly demonstrate diabetic retinal dot hemorrhage. "Calculation level 0 fundus images" and "calibration level 1 fundus images" relate to the databases DIARETDB-0 and DIARETDB-1.

1.20.3 KAGGLE Database

The Kaggle database is a public dataset containing more than 50,000 images, including medical images. The Kaggle community consists of machine learners and data scientists with diverse skills and backgrounds from all over the globe. They have a strong opinion on the research community and the field's future is brighter when they embrace distinctions. To ensure that any researcher who enjoys working with data feels equally comfortable, researchers can capture photographs.

1.20.4 Indian Diabetic Retinopathy Image Dataset (IDRiD)

An openly accessible dataset known as IDRiD was created for study and research to detect and classify Diabetic Macular Edema (DME) and Diabetic Retinopathy (DR) in retinal fundus images. A Kowa VX-10 alpha digital fundus camera, with a 50-degree field of view focused close to macula, was used to capture each of the 516 images in IDRiD collection. At 4288 × 2848 pixels, the resolution of images are saved in jpeg format. Every image has a file size of between 300 and 800 KB. This dataset includes 81 color fundus images that show DR symptoms. 27 images are utilized to assess the segmentation, while 54 images are used for training. The efficacy of individual lesion segmentation algorithms is assessed using binary masks that give precise pixel-level labeling of DR abnormalities, like microaneurysms (MA), hemorrhages (HEs), soft exudates (SE) and hard exudates (EX). The binary masks of lesions (.tiff files) that match to the color fundus images (.jpg files) are included in the dataset.

1.21 MACHINE LEARNING

The prominent example of AI in healthcare is ML, serves as foundational technique for many AI-driven healthcare technologies. It has numerous applications and implementations within the field. ML has revolutionized the healthcare sector by optimizing AI uses in medical diagnosis and treatment. The precision of this algorithm has increased at rapidly processing large volumes of clinical data, identifying and predicting patient results. Healthcare professionals are leveraging by using ML and Data Science (DS) to improve therapies and reduce costs by analyzing patient data, medical imaging, and discovering new remedies. AI technologies like machine learning enable doctors to diagnose diseases and tailor treatments with greater precision, particularly in areas such as drug research and development. Furthermore, the application of AI, especially ML in healthcare allows doctors to find previously missed connections between illnesses in patient records and recognize minute variations in physiological indicators that could be signals of possible problems.

Classical machine learning is most frequently applied in precision medicine. By identifying treatment strategies that are likely to be effective based on patients' specific profiles and treatment contexts, many healthcare organizations have made significant advancements in data science. Most AI-driven machine learning and precision medicine applications in healthcare rely on clinical data and medical imagery with known outcomes for training, a supervised learning as method.

1.22 DEEP LEARNING

Natural language processing is another approach to voice recognition in healthcare, utilizing artificial intelligence based on deep learning. However, without proper interpretation, it can be difficult to differentiate the outputs of deep learning models, as their features often hold little significance for human observers. As DL technology continues to evolve, the demand for healthcare professionals to understand and effectively apply it in clinical settings will only grow.

1.23 NATURAL LANGUAGE PROCESSING

Artificial intelligence's Natural Language Processing (NLP) field enables machines to understand and use human language. Numerous industries, including healthcare, have seen significant transformations on this technology. Personalized health care, streamlined clinical procedures, improved diagnosis accuracy and more are just a few of the many uses of NLP in health data.

NLP can be useful in extracting relevant information from health data in medical records so that diseases can be correctly diagnosed. Based on past medical data, we can also forecast future health risks and determine the best courses of action and drugs for individual patients. Furthermore, NLP offers medical professionals powerful instruments for handling vast amounts of intricate data, a process typically requiring a lot more time to perform manually.

Artificial intelligence is being used by medical professionals to diagnose diseases more precisely and give patients more individualized care and in this context, NLP is proving to be an essential tool. With time, this type of AI in healthcare will grow even more advanced and be applied in a greater range of situations. It is already quickly becoming a need in the contemporary healthcare sector.

1.24 RULE-BASED EXPERT SYSTEMS

In the 1980s and 1990s, AI technology in healthcare relied mostly on "what-if" systems. Artificial intelligence is currently employed extensively in clinical decision-making. Numerous Electronic Health Record (EHR) systems are currently in compliance with the law.

Expert systems, which are developed by engineers and experts, are predicated on a detailed set of guidelines within a specific knowledge domain. To a certain extent, these systems are effective and straightforward to comprehend and execute. But as the rules count to more than a thousand, issues develop and the system loses efficiency. Furthermore, it is challenging and time-consuming to modify accepted norms when the academic field undergoes major developments.

As a result, healthcare is moving away from traditional systems and adopting machine learning techniques that use specialized medical algorithms to interpret data.

1.25 CLASSIFIERS

Supervised Machine Learning (ML) methods implicates predicting the class for incoming data using algorithms learned on training data [18].

Support Vector Machine classifier

SVM is a ML method for the problems with two set of classification. The process creates a linear decision surface with unique properties for high generalization by mapping input vectors to a large scale of feature space. Optimization of margin in separation among classes, the machine builds up a hyperplane in a high-dimensional or infinite-dimensional. When there is no class division, optimal hyperplane minimizes the risk of classification error; support vectors are the locations closest to decision surface [19].

Decision Tree Classifier

One of the dependable methods in classification and regression is the decision tree, it is developed for effectively identifying projects as a non-parametric supervised learning strategy. Gathering rules from straightforward decision rules and properties of the dataset is one of the key goals of this part. Learning basic decision rules and information gleaned from data features can also be done using decision trees. Decision-making will involve speaking and taking into account learning capabilities. One way to classify a decision tree is to consider its root to leaf nodes while sorting and gathering information about the tree. Mostly, the instance that is being taken from the system is the subject of the entire classification.

Random forest classifier

An essential supervised classification method for algorithms, random forest is useful to get things started. The main purpose of random forests is to construct forests and take into account many trees. Additionally, the forest will be taken into mind and a strong culture for trees will be created. The random forest classifier will be helpful in this and provide tree numbers to apply more accuracy in developing the results.

Linear regression classifier

The linear regression algorithm, which creates a coefficient to minimize residual square sums, is another significant technique. It can also be utilized to make accurate predictions and be observed with targets.

Activation function:

- **Sigmoid**: For a real-valued input, the sigmoid function yields a value midst 0 and 1 (equation 1.1).

$$f_{sigmoid}(t) = \frac{1}{1+e^{-t}} \quad (1.1)$$

- **Algebraic Sigmoid**: This function returns a value in the interval [1, 1] given an input of real numbers (equation 1.2).

$$f_{asigmoid}(t) = \frac{t}{\sqrt{1+t^2}} \quad (1.2)$$

- **Tanh**: Utilizing the hyperbolic tangent function, it limits the input to the interval [1, 1] (equation 1.3).

$$f_{Tanh}(t) = \frac{e^{-}-e}{e^{t}+e^{-t}} \quad (1.3)$$

- **Rectified Linear Unit**: A ReLU function sets the negative value of input to 0 while keeping positive value as constant (equation 1.4).

$$f_{ReLu}(t) = max(0, t) \quad (1.4)$$

- **Noisy ReLU**: The noisy version of ReLU uses a Gaussian distribution sample, whose variance relies on positive input value sigmoid (t), and mean is 0 (equation 1.5).

$$f_{n\_rel}(t) = max(0, t+\varepsilon), \varepsilon \sim N(0, \sigma(t)) \quad (1.5)$$

- **Leaky ReLU**: As opposed to producing a zero value, a leaky ReLU function produces a scaled-down version of the negative input (equation 1.6).

$$f_{l\_rel}(t) = \{t \quad if\ t > 0ct \quad if\ t \leq 0\} \qquad (1.6)$$

- **Randomized ReLU**: In the leaky ReLU function, the leak factor is randomly chosen by using the randomized leaky ReLU (RReLU), a leaky Rectifier Linear Unit (equation 1.7).

$$f_{r\_rel}(t) = \{t \quad if\ t > 0at \quad if\ t \leq 0\} \qquad (1.7)$$

- **Exponential Linear Units (ELU):** Since an exponential linear unit's value can be either positive or negative, its goal is to reduce the mean activations to zero (equation 1.8).

$$f_{r\_rel}(t) = \{t \quad if\ t > 0at \quad if\ t \leq 0\} \qquad (1.8)$$

Pooling layers have an impact on the feature map, using maximum, minimum, or average functions. The stride length determines output feature map size, whereas pooled image size is governed by pooling window size.

Pooling layer in the network is used to reduce the number and computation of parameters as well as generated feature maps' spatial size representation. The following is a summary of main functions [20–22] of pooling layers:

a. Extraction of Invariant Features

b. Dimensionality and Parameter Reduction

c. Computational Cost Reduction

d. Controls Over-fitting

Optimization for back propagation (BP)

In neural networks, the weight updater is a BP, which updates weights by optimizing the values to achieve desired outcome. SGD is typically employed for this optimization [23–24]. SGD is an iterative optimization technique that evaluates the gradient values using shuffled samples. Since SGD uses random probability to choose samples, it can occasionally produce a noisy path from standard gradient descent algorithms to the endpoint because unpredictability may need a few more rounds. However, this algorithm's low computing cost makes it appropriate for use. Adam is an additional optimizer type that may be utilized in place of this SGD. This optimizer requires relatively little memory and can handle huge problems with many variables and data. It is also suitable for problems with noisy gradients and non-stationary targets [25]. Another optimizer that uses gradient updates in a moving window is called Adadelta. Instead of accumulating the gradients from the past, learning keeps updated [26]. The trio of optimizers in question is the ones selected for testing.

1.26 THE SCOPE AND OBJECTIVES OF THE WORK

- The primary aim of this research is to create an automated method for DR detection.

- Creating a method using Deep Learning to accurately detect and classify DR existence and the severity levels, allowing for early detection and improved patient outcomes.

- This research work is based on the method for early detection of Dot Hemorrhages (DH) with the best accuracy, enhancing the image's sensitivity in the retina using dynamic image comparison techniques.

- The study aims to create an AI model using trained datasets to classify fundus images from different datasets and hospitals.

- The algorithm extracts pixels, color profiles and rendering indications for images providing accurate results in a short time.

- In the present study, an efficient algorithm and techniques is used for optimal accuracy in identifying the dot hemorrhages in order to increase the image's sensitivity (an image taken using a 20D lens) in order to enhance by comparative analysis of dynamic dot hemorrhages.

- It can be concluded that the time needed to diagnose the retina accurately, efficiently, and precisely will be shortened by comparing the 400 million pixel image in three seconds with the predicted image using the suggested technique, 48 megapixels in less than 300–500 milliseconds and 45 million pixels in one second. Both patients and doctors can benefit from this method's ability to shorten turnaround times and deliver accurate results more quickly in clinical diagnostic settings.

1.27 MOTIVATION

- DR is among the main factors that lead to blindness and is becoming more widespread globally. Early diagnosis and treatment can lower the chance of blindness.
- The current methods are efficient, but they require a lot of resources.
- Building an automated DR screening system is essential.
- It is recommended that all diabetic patients undergo eye exams at least once a year, preferably every six months.
- Any automatic rapid screening method or tool would be beneficial for individuals with this disease and reduce the need for skilled human sources.

This dissertation aims to analyze changes in the ocular vascular system during diabetes progression from diabetes to retinopathy using computational vision, machine learning and data analysis methods. The dissertation also explores genetic image comparison techniques and algorithms for studying retinal dot hemorrhages simultaneously and in various theoretical frameworks. It also examines distinct clusters of retinal cells to identify more potent biomarkers. The dissertation evaluates biomarkers, retinal features and machine learning methods in synergistic contexts to consider individual changes over time and potential diagnostic possibilities for various disease phases.

1.28 THESIS ORGANIZATION CHART

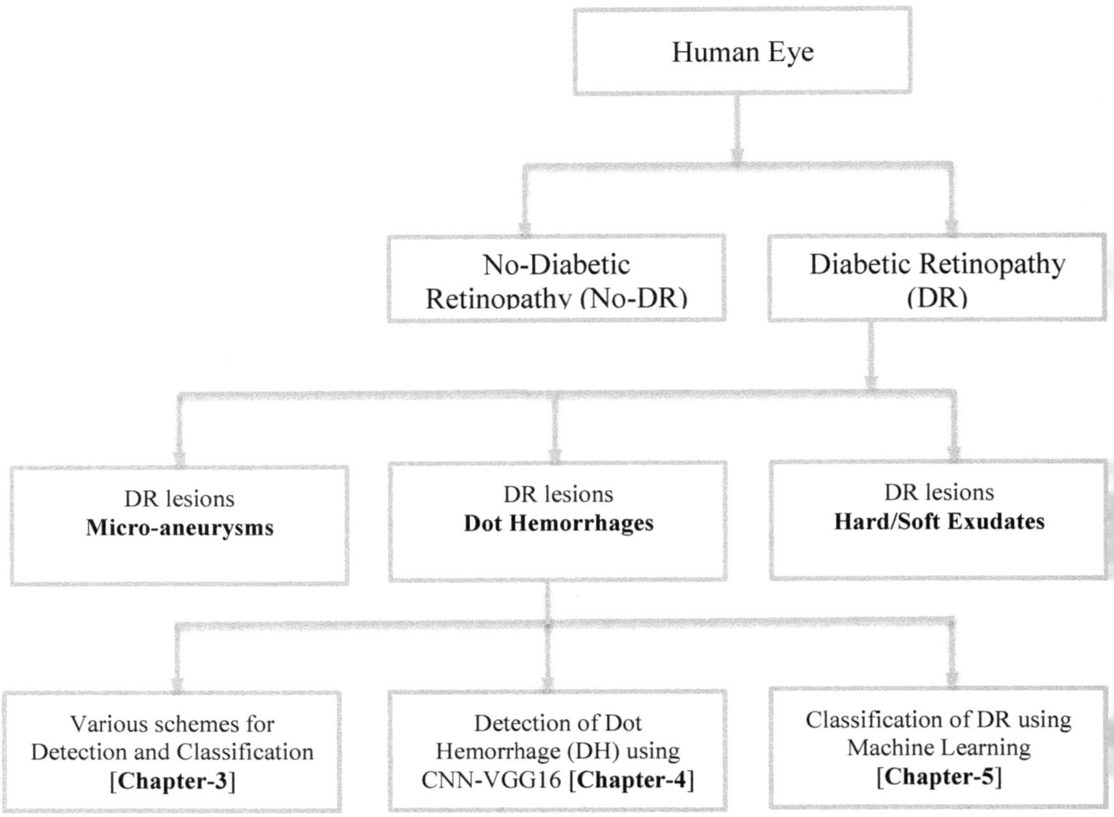

Figure 1.9 An outline of the suggested method

CHAPTER 2

LITERATURE SURVEY

2.1 INTRODUCTION

Diabetic retinopathy is greatest enduring side effects of diabetes and key contributor to vision loss worldwide. A condition known as vitreous hemorrhages, which result in hard exudates and cotton wool patches on the retina, are caused by abnormal blood vessel proliferation. Early diagnosis of the illness is essential to preventing blindness and automated DR classification helps achieve. Many attempts have been made to create a programmed automatic system that can classify several stages of this DR illness. This literature review chapter explores several ML techniques and NN architectures on classification of DR using retinal fundus images. Many technologies have been developed to automatically detect the diabetic retinopathy using fundus images.

In this part, several techniques for identifying and categorizing ocular conditions linked to diabetic retinopathy are thoroughly reviewed. It provides an in-depth analysis of Deep Learning (DL) and ML methods for DR identification and classification.

2.2 VARIOUS METHODS ARE USED FOR THE DETECTION AND CLASSIFICATION OF EARLY DOT HEMORRHAGES IN DIABETIC RETINAL DISEASE

An ANN classifier is used to provide the best results in regard to precision and sensitivity [27] regarding the DR classification, utilizing resilient backpropagation methods and Bayesian regularization. In [28], a novel Modified Hopfield Neural Network (MHNN) is employed to demonstrate applicability for the anomaly categorization from human retinal pictures for DR. Many experiments with various ANN types have been proposed and conducted. However, because of its advanced performances, all the technical approaches uses DL when it appears on screen. The literature overview of classification methods that use DL models like CNN is more specifically covered in the parts that follow.

The automatic screening method developed by N. Gharaibeh et al. [29] produced a 98.4% accuracy rate in the DR classification after a sequence of prior to processing techniques, CNN is employed for feature extraction, selection and classification. Retinal images are converted into entropy images to enrich classification. Quantification of an image information indicates the complexity of original fundus images. After that, classification is carried out using DL, which raises the accuracy to 86.0% from 81.8% when utilizing standard fundus images.

Another study in [30] achieves 86.17% accuracy using CNN and SVM as the classifier. In this case, the model is built on SVM, CNN, fractional max-pooling and an optimization method based on learning. VGG-19, a Visual Geometry Group Network (VGGNet) uses a pre-processing tasks, is employed for classification of DR [31]. This classification method uses singular value decomposition for feature selection and Gaussian mixture for region segmentation. The proposed model is claimed to yield better results, with a 98.34% accuracy efficiency in DL-based segmentation, feature extraction, feature selection, and classification.

Zhang W. et al [32] conducted an additional experiment wherein transfer learning and ensemble learning are employed in the DL model to classify DR images. Data augmentation is applied after pre-processing methods like histogram equalization and picture normalization. An average accuracy of 96.50% is attained by the model.

A longstanding goal of AI in ophthalmology has been to develop computerized screening using retinal images (Abramoff et al. 2016; Abramoff et al. 2008). CNN just underwent DR screening training, and it performed on par with a team of qualified ophthalmologists. (Gulshan et al. 2016). Analyzing retinal images from sizable, ethnically diverse patient populations with diabetes produced results that were very high in relation to specificity and sensitivity. In addition to verified the efficacy and affordability of DR screening with three commercially available software tools. (Tufail et al. 2017).

Rajpurkar et al. (2017) presented a U-net framework with skip links for segmenting images from one to another. Optimizing pre-trained VGG networks and eliminating specialized layers significantly refines the Deep Retinal Image Understanding technique. This encourages research into supervised deep learning techniques.

A modified U-net design was used by Fu et al. (2018) to develop a Multidimensional network for OD-OC segmentation. Before submitting RGB fundus images and the segmentation map into the network, they underwent Polar Transformation (PT). An inverse PT was then applied to the results. While the use of PT yielded innovative outcomes, the network is not end-to-end in its very nature.

The automated DH grading approach proposed by Zaki et al. (2016) was well received by clinicians. It was employed to identify irregularities in retinal images and assess patient retinal conditions using fundus images. An efficient evaluation process was developed to provide ophthalmologists with an additional perspective during diagnosis. Various automated DH grading methods were implemented to complement manual assessments. Blood vascular tortuosity, a key feature linked to the stages of diabetic hemorrhages, was measured for grading purposes. Vascular segmentation improved the accuracy and efficiency of the process while maintaining precision.

2.3 DETECTION OF DIABETIC RETINAL DOT HEMORRHAGE USING DYNAMIC IMAGE COMPARISON WITH DEEP NEURAL NETWORKS

In the case of DR, this section suggests detecting dot hemorrhages using various Neural Networks architectures to obtain enhanced accuracy.

Siamese-like CNN architecture is designed to accommodate simultaneous binocular fundus images for patient prediction in each eye. The model incorporates pre-processing techniques like data augmentation and transfer learning make it more effective. For the green channel extraction-based DR classification of fundus images, Shanthi T. et al. employed an AlexNet CNN as a pre-processing method [33]. Kathiresan S. et al. [34] suggested a Synergic DL technique, which resulted in accurate classification for DR classification of fundus images. The DL model has a better classification accuracy than numerous other models already in use when pre-processing and segmentation are carried out prior to classification. After utilizing CNN to extract the features of a distinct research by Gayathri S. et al. [35] classifies DR using many ML classifiers and produces extremely good results. In this experiment, the integration of several classifiers with CNN proves to be an excellent classifier.

Multi-scale shallow CNN is combined in another experiment [36]. Every CNN is used as a foundational learner that facilitates feature extraction across a range of perceptual domains relevant to vision and the networks' integration is used to determine the final classification. When compared to other cutting-edge models, the integrated method demonstrates its superior performance. The model performs better when other picture improvement methods are used, such as histogram equalization and unsharp masking (UM). In the study by Pao S.I. et al. [37], the fundus image preprocessing and the entropy of the gray level fundus images are assessed using UM. Better results are obtained when a bichannel CNN incorporates both picture formats for classification.

The fundus image data is subjected to contrast limited adaptive histogram equalization and histogram equalization approach in [38] to allow CNN's DR classification. The CNN DenseNet121 pretrained architecture is used by Chaturvedi S.S. et al. [39] for fundus image classification, with the Pooling, Dropout and Softmax layers coming next. This method proved to be accurate and efficient in computing time and space by using fine-tuning and transfer learning to Prospective research recommendations are provided together with an evaluation and discussion of pertinent issues. Inspired by Shao et al. (2018) classification framework, the Adaptive Migration Biogeography-Based Optimization (AMBBO) approach was created for the categorization of fundus images. The AMBBO-based RBFN neural network is used in this method for classification and the study of FIQAINS model is used to evaluate the fundus image quality.

2.4 USING MACHINE LEARNING TECHNIQUES, A CLASSIFICATION OF VARIOUS STAGES OF DIABETIC RETINOPATHY (DR)

Classifying an image involves choosing it from a predetermined set of categories, for which many methods have been developed. A widely employed technique in a variety of fields is machine learning. Fundus images are used for classifying Diabetic Retinopathy using ML methods. In [40], the analysis of classifying DR images and non-DR images using a three-stage classification. The three stages of DR processing-segmentation, lesion categorization, and severity grading-are handled by machine learning techniques such as AdaBoost, k-nearest neighbor (KNN), Support Vector Machines (SVM) and Gaussian Mixture Model (GMM). It is discovered that KNN and GMM excel in the classification.

SVM and KNN are utilized to detect retinal microaneurysms by the classification [41] of DR using Messidor and DBret datasets, with

SVM outperforming KNN. SVM performs better than Decision Trees and Logistic Regression when it comes to DR prediction [42]. SVM is primarily utilized in numerous DR classifications, demonstrating its effectiveness in obtaining excellent results [41-44]. SVM is utilized for DR categorization into three classes-normal, mild and severe-followed by pre-processing and segmentation [45].

An analysis [46] comparing two ML methods for classification of DR cases shows the Naive Bayes classifier performs better than SVM. Because random forest approaches exceed logistic regression, they are recommended as a useful tool for diagnosing DR [47]. Three models-SVM, Bayesian classification and Probabilistic Neural Network (PNN)-are utilized in [48] for DR classification; SVM performs better than the other two. In an additional study [49], multilayer perceptron neural networks are employed to detect DR in retinal images.

ML for classification of DR by means of particular retinal images was studied by Ahmed Almulihi, Malik Bader Alazzam and Fawaz Alassery [50]. To categorize retinal images based on the presence or absence of disease-related retinopathy, they utilized models of Optimal Path Forest (OPF) and Restricted Boltzmann Machines (RBM). Gayathri et al. suggested an automated model for binary and multiclass categorization of DR [51]. Retinal fundus pictures were utilized to extract features using the Anisotropic Dual-Tree Complex Wavelet Transform (ADTCWT). An automated DR screening approach using machine learning techniques was presented by K. K. Mujeeb Rahman, Ahmed Imran, Mohamed Nasor, et al. [52]. DNN and SVM were the two techniques used. Image segmentation, feature extraction and classification were the three main processes that were highlighted in the study. The goal of Narayanan et al.'s [53] mixed ML architecture to diagnose and grade DR. The utilization of popular networks including VGG16, AlexNet, ResNet, DenseNet, NASNet, GoogleNet and Inception-v3 for transfer learning-based DR identification was also examined in this study. Throughout the grading process, they employed principal component analysis, CNN fusion and an SVM classifier to lower the dimensionality.

Image processing methods were used to discover abnormalities in retinal images to lower the cost of screenings. Exudates were routinely checked they were frequently studied as markers of diabetic retinopathy. Jadhav et al. [54] first reported NPDR, a condition with symptoms resembling those of type 1 diabetes. Using an image-based segmentation method for feature extraction, the exudate feature was detected.

An automated method for evaluating diabetic maculopathy was developed by Ramasamy et al. [55], which can help ophthalmic to diagnose disorders. The orientation of the optic disc and its vascular composition were used in suggested method to separate the macula from a digitized retinal image. For every exudate area, binary maps with filter banks and feature vectors were produced. Based on macula coordinates and exudate properties, a classifier based on the GMM to categorize retinal images into several phases of maculopathy. Nevertheless, no discernible grading of the digitized retinal images was noticed.

Using image processing techniques, A method for detecting and measuring diabetic retinopathy lesions was created by Patwari et al. (2013). Lesions that were visible after angiography were marked on the processed fundus images. The procedure started with high-resolution fundus images, which were then enhanced using methods such as intensity transformation and histogram equalization to carry out morphological procedures and detect microaneurysms. Segmentation was then used to define the boundaries of detected microaneurysms. The sensitivity rate didn't alter even with better resolution. In a parallel endeavor, Rahim et al. (2016) presented a unique automated screening technique for DR that aims to determine the retinopathy's early symptoms.

Athitsos et al. introduced a method to distinguish computer-generated images from real photographs by analyzing the visual content and geometric features of the images. This approach utilizes an algorithm that employs multiple decision trees as a classifier. The assessment sample for this technique consisted of 1,025 computer-generated images and 643 photographic images. An Ada Boosting learning classifier was used by Chen et al. to determine whether a picture was created by a computer or by photography, on furthest neighbor histogram feature. The dataset used to train this model included 36,000 computer-generated images and 35,000 manually taken images.

Table 2.1 Literature summary

Sl No.	Authors	Year	Methods employed	Dataset	Remarks
1	Zhang, Q.Met al., [32]	2021	CNN and Cuckoo search for segmentation, feature extraction, and feature optimization	MESSIDOR and IDRiD	Accuracy
2	Jadhav, Ambaji S. et al. [54]	2021	Rider Optimization Algorithm based on Modified Gear and Steering and Deep Belief Network (MGS-ROA)	DIARETDB1	Accuracy
3	L K Ramasamyet al., [55]	2021	Sequential Minimal Optimization and the Ridgelet Transform	Kaggle & DIARETDB1	Kaggle dataset: Accuracy DIARETDB1 Accuracy
4	Jayanthi, J. et al., [56]	2021	Particle swarm Optimization, CNN and Decision tree	MESSIDOR	Accuracy
5	Kathiresan S.et al. [34]	2020	Segmentation model based on histograms and classification model based on SDLs	MESSIDOR	Accuracy
6	Chen W. et al., [36]	2020	Fusion of several shallow scales CNN	Kaggle	Accuracy

Table 2.1 (Continued)

Sl No.	Authors	Year	Methods employed	Dataset	Remarks
7	Gayathri S.et al., [35]	2020	CNN is utilized for feature extraction, while ML models like SVM, AdaBoost, Naive Bayes and Random Forest are employed for classification.	IDRiD, MESSIDOR, and KAGGLE	Binary and multiclass classification
8	Hemanth D.J. et al., [38]	2020	Histogram equalization and Contrast limited adaptive histogram equalization are two related concepts.	MESSIDOR	Accuracy
9	Shanthi T.et al., [33]	2019	Modified Alexnet architecture	MESSIDOR	Accuracy
10	Mateen M. et al., [57]	2019	Singular value decomposition (SVD), GMM, VGG-19 DNN and principal component analysis (PCA)	Kaggle	Accuracy
11	Li Y.H. et al., [58]	2019	CNN, SVM, fractional max pooling and a learning-based optimization technique	Kaggle	Accuracy
12	Lin G.M. et al., [59]	2018	CNN classification and transformed entropy images	Kaggle	Accuracy
13	Gharaibeh N. et al., [29]	2018	Classification and feature extraction with CNN	DIARETDB1	Accuracy

Table 2.1 (Continued)

Sl No.	Authors	Year	Methods employed	Dataset	Remarks
14	Lam C. et al., [30]	2018	CNN with preprocessing, augmentation and feature extraction	Messidor MildDR	Accuracy
15	Adem K., [31]	2018	CNN for classification, segmentation and preprocessing	DIARETDB0, DIARETDB1, DIARETDB	Accuracy
16	Wan S. et al., [60]	2018	Different CNN architectures, transfer learning, hyper parameter tweaking, normalization and augmentation	Kaggle dataset	Accuracy
17	Tsao H.Y et.al., [42]	2018	SVM model	Real time images	Accuracy and AUC
18	Carrera E.V., et.al., [43]	2018	SVM model	400 retinal images	Sensitivity
19	Gargeya R et.al., [61]	2017	Pre-processing, Data augmentation with Deep Learning	MESSIDOR 2 E-Ophtha	AUC
20	Xu K., et.al., [62]	2017	Data augmentation with CNN architecture	Kaggle dataset	Accuracy
21	García G., et.al., [63]	2017	VGG net based CNN architecture	EyePACS	Accuracy

Table 2.1 (Continued)

Sl No.	Authors	Year	Methods employed	Dataset	Remarks
22	Pratt H., et.al., [64]	2016	CNN with data augmentation	Kaggle dataset	Specificity, Accuracy, Sensitivity
23	B. Antal et.al., [65]	2012	Ensemble-based framework	Messidor database	AUC
24	Lachure J., et.al.,[41]	2015	KNN and Support Vector Machine (SVM) classifiers	Messidor database	Specificity, Sensitivity for SVM.
25	Roychowdhury S., et.al., [40]	2014	GMM and kNN classifiers	Messidor database	Sensitivity, Specificity, and AUC
26	Mansour R.F., et.al., [44]	2013	SVM model	1200 retinal images	Sensitivity, Specificity
27	Aravind C., et.al., [45]	2013	SVM model	Real time images	Sensitivity, Specificity
28	M. Niemeijer et.al., [66]	2005	The k-NN classifier is utilized in conjunction with morphological approaches for classification.	Messidor database	Sensitivity, Specificity

2.5 SUMMARY

This chapter presents the diabetic retinal dot hemorrhage-related research projects that have been undertaken. A number of authors discuss various techniques for detecting dot hemorrhage that can be used to increase the identification rate while reducing the complexity. These methods include neural networks that employ the K-nearest neighbor algorithm, K-means clustering, decision trees, support vector machines, hidden Markov models, CNN, LSTM, PSTM, ensemble and other deep neural network methods. To shorten the computation time and accelerate the identification procedure, the author also discusses various image preprocessing techniques, segmentation and feature selection methods like mean filter, median filter, random forest selection, genetic algorithm, and ant colony based feature selection. Thus, the strategies are useful for accurately and with a low error rate classifying the various types of hemorrhages. Additionally, the process can be used to evaluate the extents of a certain category of extrusions or mishaps with great precision. Our proposed method divides an image into two sections, with the audience selecting the superior one. An algorithm is utilized to create a model for assessing the severity of diabetic retinal hemorrhage. This procedure allows the ophthalmologist a streamlined way to examine the samples without obstructing their vision of the eye and creates the impression that the exam is being done clearly.

CHAPTER 3

VARIOUS SCHEMES FOR DETECTING AND CLASSIFYING EARLY DOT HEMORRHAGES IN DIABETIC RETINAL DISEASE

3.1 INTRODUCTION

Dot hemorrhage is a benign form of retinal disease that requires regular screening in diabetic patients to prevent vision loss. Initially, it lacks a significant effect on vision, but as disease progresses, it causes blindness. Early detection and treatment are necessary to preclude blindness in patient. Manually examining each patient is costly and time-consuming. The automated diagnosis system can detect early symptoms of conditions such as dot hemorrhage by utilizing sophisticated medical imaging techniques. Identification of these abnormalities would aid in the immediate treatment and prevention of blindness, thereby contributing to an improvement in life quality.

The majority of methods described in the literature employ dynamic pre-processing of images obtained from patients with dilated pupils. The dot hemorrhages are plainly visible, but their intrusive nature causes patients greater discomfort. To surmount these limitations, the current study develops automatic detection of dot hemorrhage. Operation with multiple features and sequential classifiers that enhance precision. This system precisely removes blood vessels and extracts all dark lesions like dot hemorrhage.

3.2 METHODS FOR DETECTING AND CLASSIFYING FOR DIABETIC RETINOPATHY USING DOT HEMORRHAGES

Across a wide range of medical applications, deep neural networks offer a potent tool that aids medical professionals in the analysis, modeling and understanding of complex clinical data. Back Propagation Algorithms, which are gradient-based techniques, are preferred by the vast majority of applications in the field of artificial computing for NN training. The input stage, hidden stage and output stage are the three stages that make up an average neural network, according to Figure 3.1. NN receives a feature vector derived from input retina image. During testing phase, network is completed in an extensive range of retinal images to efficiently identify whether or not an individual has diabetes. The neural network requires two steps in order to operate: training and testing. Neural networks are utilized to detect diabetic retinal disease after phase segmentation and information extraction. The primary focus of diabetic retinal disease diagnosis is feature extraction of blood vessels, optical disks, and damage areas. The neural network requires two steps in order to operate: training and testing. Neural networks are utilized to detect diabetic retinal disease after phase segmentation and information extraction. The primary focus of diabetic retinal disease diagnosis is feature extraction of blood vessels, optical disks, and damage areas. That procedure has to be automated, which calls for a clever system that can handle it effectively. A CNN using ANN model utilized in this thesis to accomplish the objectives. CNN is a broadly used DL architecture in a computing. Artificial intelligence's computer vision subfield makes it possible for a computer to understand and analyze visual data or images.

ANNs work remarkably well in ML technique. They are widely used across various types of datasets, incorporating images, audio and text. To estimate the expression order, recurrent neural networks, specifically LSTMs, are employed. Similarly, CNN are used for image classification. The essential components of a CNN will be developed in this study. Neural networks typically consist of three types of layers:

1) Data is fed into the model through input layer, the quantity of neurons in an image is correlated with its characteristics or overall pixel count.

2) Data are sent from the input layer to the hidden layer. The model in addition to amount of data can have an effect on the number of hidden layers. There could be a variation in the number of neurons in each buried layer but overall, neurons outnumber features. Nonlinearity is introduced in each network layer by multiplying the output of previous layer by learnable weights, adding biases and then applying an activation function.

3) At output layer, the data is processed using a logistic function like softmax or sigmoid to convert it into a more interpretable form for probability ratings in each class. The subsequent process, known as feed forward, involves inputting data into the model and generating outputs for each layer. The network's performance is subsequently assessed using an error function, like cross-entropy or loss mean squared error. This error factor helps measure the network's efficiency. Afterward, derivatives are computed and backpropagation is applied to the model to minimize loss. CNNs, an advancement over traditional artificial

NN, are widely used to extract features from datasets with grid structures, such as images. CNNs are particularly useful for both static and dynamic visual datasets where recognizing data patterns is crucial. The pooling, FC layers, convolutional and input layers are significant levels of the CNN model.

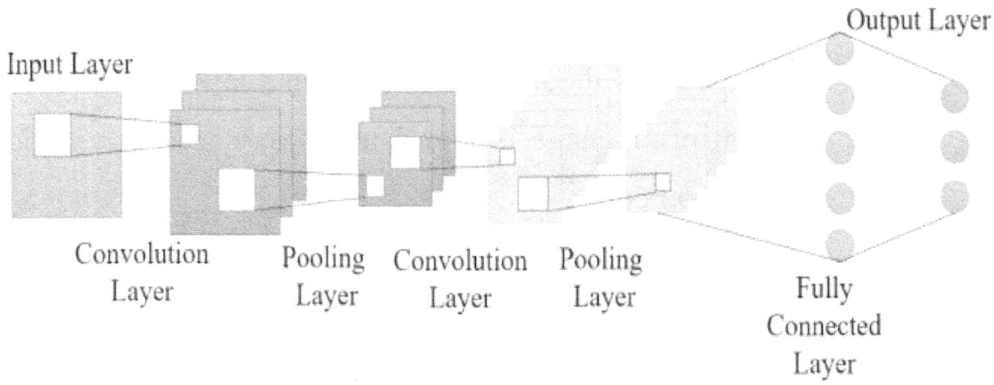

Figure 3.1 CNN design model

To identify and extract the features out of the input image, convolutional layer applies filters. The final prediction is generated by FC layer after pooling layer has reduced the size of input image, thereby decreasing computational complexity. Through gradient descent and backpropagation, the network acquires optimal filters.

Networks of neurons that share parameters are referred to as convnets or convolutional neural networks. RGB channels that are commonly seen in the images may be used to represent it as a cuboid that has three measurements: height, breadth and length.

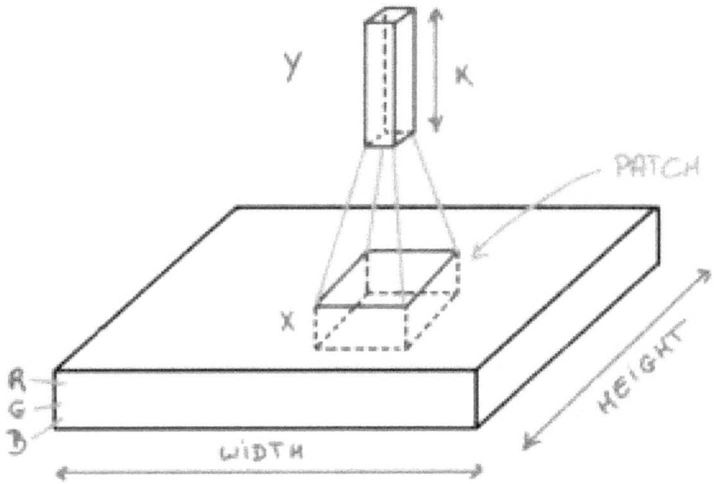

Figure 3.2 Cuboid representation of an image with k outputs

Imagine applying a kernel or filter - a small neural networks -to a specific region of the image and then the results are displayed vertically with K outputs. The neural network will generate a new set of image with updated characteristics like heights, widths and pits as it traverses whole image. The extra channels depicted in Figure 3.2 are taller and narrower compared to original RGB channels and this process is referred to convolution. Neural network will function as predicted if the patch size and image size match. By concentrating on the smaller region, this method lowers the total number of weights.

Math is involved throughout the whole convolution process. Kernels are a collection of filters that may be adjusted via learning with small heights, widths and depths that corresponds to the input volume (or three if the input is an image) make up convolution layers. For example, an image with the size 34x34x3 might use convolution. If 'a' is smaller than the image dimension, it can have a value between 3 and 7. In this case, the filter's size would be a*a*3. While progressing through forward pass, each filter is gradually moved across the input volume, we compute the dot product by multiplying the kernel weights with the relevant patch of the input volume. The stride, which might be two, three, or even four for high-definition images, defines the action.

Each filter has a 2-D output that may be produced by sliding it. By stacking filters, an output dimension will be generated with a depth that is proportional to number of filters. Convents are built using layers. An architecture of Convolution Neural Networks that is more complete is called Convnets. A differentiable function is used in each layer of a CNN to transform a volume into another.

Different layer: For example, consider an image with dimensions of 224 × 224. The model receives data input at the input layer. A single or a set of images may often be fed into a CNN.

Activation Layer: The non-linearity to the network has been introduced by activation layers to produce the preceding layer output. Convolution layer output from the element will get activated by activation function like RELU, Leaky RELU, max (0, x) and Tanh. The dimension of 224 × 224 retains the output volume that remains unchanged during the course.

Pooling layer:

This layer, often added to Convnets, primarily aims to reduce the volume. This helps speed up computation, save memory and mitigate overfitting. Average and Max pooling are two widely used methods of pooling. After being flattened, the feature maps from pooling and convolution layers are transformed into vectors in one dimension, for regression or classification tasks, as shown in Figure 3.3, to be sent to FC layer.

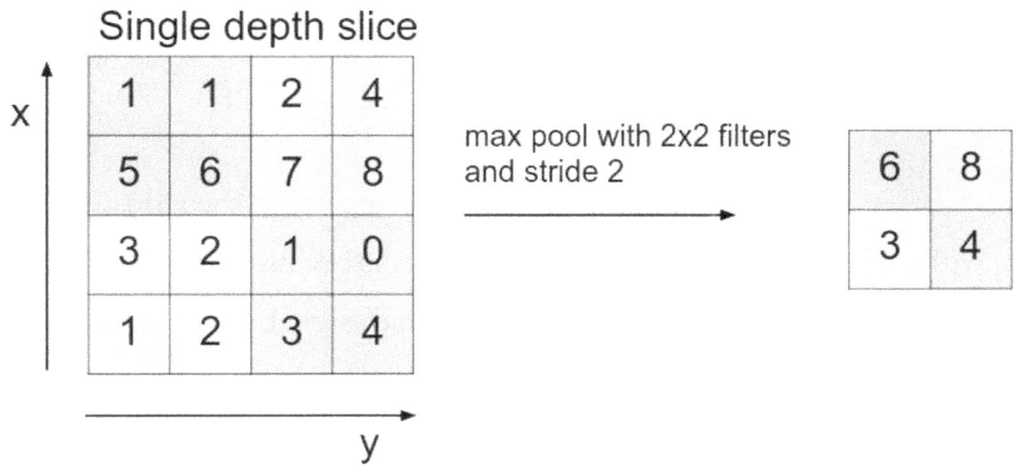

Figure 3.3 Filtered portion of image

Fully connected layer: After FC layers, the output is run via logistic function for classification like softmax or sigmoid. The output for every class is converted by this function into a probability score for that class.

Pre-trained model undergone training using certain type of datasets that includes many classes. Pre-trained CNN models are now available for the Image Net database, which has 1.3 million images organized into 1000 distinct classes. It is not necessary to train the first few layers of a CNN model to apply it for different visual recognition tasks that has been trained on a similar, big scale issue, like Image Net. Fixed feature detectors are those fixed layers that aren't employed in training.

The top layers might be modified to better suit the current problem of the technique of classifying eye conditions like diabetic retinopathy refers to transfer learning. Taking into account that the system employed a CNN trained on a pertinent but unrelated issue. Large training datasets are not always necessary when using transfer learning to speed up learning.

If transfer learning is used in comparable scenarios, the CNN will adjust to the new task rather well. This is because natural stimuli, like visual recognition, contain compositional signals, which are signals composed of simpler signals. For visual recognition tasks, each ConvNet's early layers will learn roughly identical "basis" components such as edge, color, or gradient features.

With the help of the Image Net dataset, several CNN models been trained. This chapter explains the architectural features of pretrained CNN in OCT/Fundus image captioning and image classification.

3.3 VGG-16 MODEL

VGG16 is a model of CNN created at the University of Oxford. This model uses the 15 million images from 1000 classes in the ImageNet dataset to achieve an accuracy rate of 93% in top-5 tests. VGG16 as one of prominent models utilized in the ILSVRC-2014 findings. By deleting huge kernel-sized filters and substituting numerous smaller 3*3 kernel-sized filters, this model outperforms AlexNet.

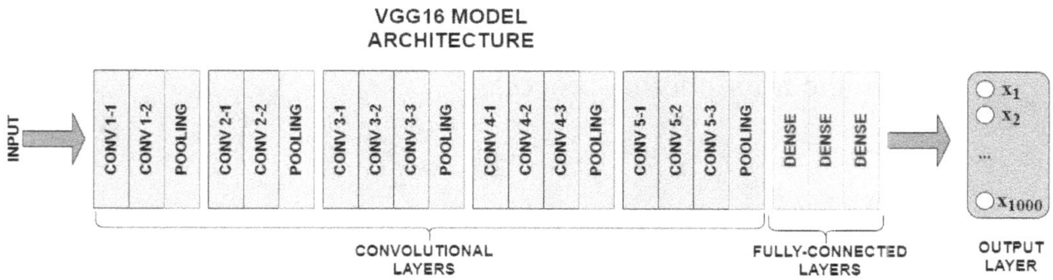

Figure 3.4 VGG16 Model Architecture

NVIDIA's Titan Black GPU was utilized for the purpose of training the VGG16 model. In Figure 3.4 depicts VGG16 layered simplified architecture, which includes all of the layers, their respective sizes for input & output and other architectural details.

The number of layers whose weights may be trained is indicated by the number 16 in VGG16. Throughout training, the weights of the thirteen convolutional layers, it is possible to modify two fully/completely connected and one dense layer. RGB image has a constant size of 224 × 224 pixels is sent into the convolution stage. To convolve with an input image, in a sequence convolutional layers is used, each employing filters with a 33 receptive field. Eleven convolution filters are used in one of the setups. This filter's input channels appear to be linearly modified.

Activation is done using RELU which is a non-linear function. A fixed pixel of 1 is used for the convolution step. Spatial padding for convolution is carefully adjusted to maintain the spatial resolution following convolution. Applying a padding of 1 pixel for 33 convolution will allow you to keep the spatial resolution after the convolution is finished. After several convolutional layers, 5 Max pooling layers are employed. A window with dimensions of 224 pixels by 224 stride is used to perform the Max-pooling process.

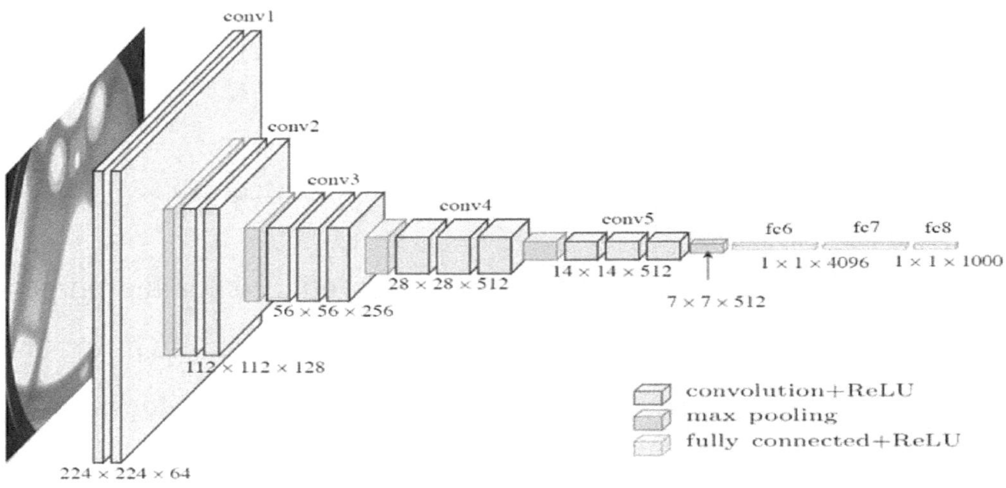

Figure 3.5 Pre-trained VGG16 Model Complete Architecture

Three FC layers follow the convolutional layer stack. The initial two FC connected layers each contain 4096 units. Considering this model needs to classify 1000 distinct classes, the third fully connected layer contains 1000 units. As shown in Figure 3.5, the softmax layer is the last one used for classification. In several multilayer neural networks, the output of the penultimate layer is real-valued scores. Real valued scores are highly challenging to work with and very tough to comfortably scale.

3.4 VGG-19 MODEL

At University of Oxford, VG Group developed the CNN VGG-19 using ImageNet dataset. The RGB picture (224, 224) is also included in the input for the VGG19 network. In VGG19, there are 19 trainable layers each and every convolution layer employs two filters

(3, 3) and increase the power of two, more filters are used in each block (64, 128, 256, 512). The term Conv3-64 designates 64 unique square with the filters have dimensions of 3 by 3. Convolutional layers with a stride length of one pixel in length and one pixel of padding on each side. There are five sets of convolution layers: two layers with 64 filters in the first set, two levels with 128 filters in the second set, third set has four levels of 256 filters and four layers of 512 filters in each of last two sets. Between every set of convolution layers, there is a maximum number of pooling layers. The 2*2 filters are applied with a stride of 2 (pixels) for maximum pooling layers.

A flattening procedure is used to the last pooling layer before it is transferred up to 4096 neurons in FC layer. The output routed to a second fully linked layer that has 4096 neurons. Next, a third layer receives the result of this layer is a fully linked layer consisting of 1000 neurons. Every one of these levels is activated by the RELU activation function. Using cross entropy loss, the Softmax layer forecasts the probability for a thousand distinct classes. Figure 3.6 displays the pre-trained model's entire architecture VGG19.

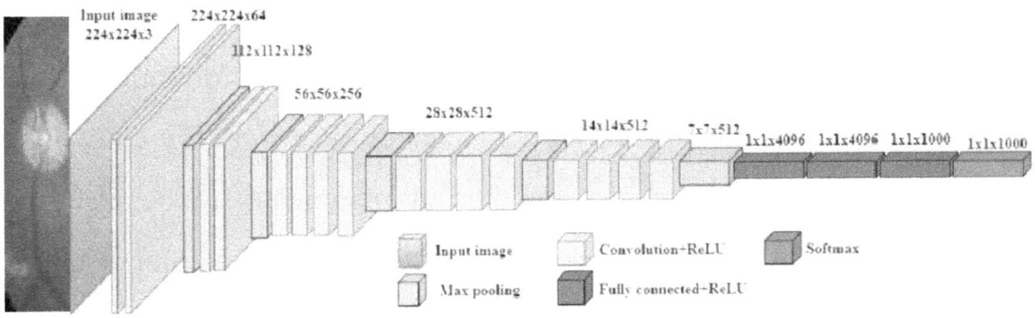

Figure 3.6 VGG19 Model Architecture

The number 19 indicates how many layers have their weights changed during training. There are trainable weights for each of the sixteen convolutional layers including three fully connected layers. To train VGG-19, the ImageNet challenge (ILSVRC) for classifying 1000 different types of classes was utilized.

3.5 INCEPTION IMAGES

The Inception Pre-trained model comes in three main varieties. The sort of convolution employed will vary between them.

3.5.1 Convolution Factorization

Convolutions are factorized into smaller convolutions to decrease the number of parameters and connections without performance degrading. The efficacy of the system is contingent upon the amount of parameters that these layers must acquire one layer with a 55 filter is employed is 5*5=25. The overall count of characteristics that require learning is (3 * 3 + 3 * 3=18) if there are two layers of 3*3 filters. As a result, 28% fewer parameters are required. Two 3*3 convolution filters were employed in Inception Module-A to minimize the number of characteristics that require learning asymmetrical transformation Once 33 convolution is used in place of a 31 convolution and a 13 convolution. Three filters in threes (33), number of parameters to be discovered is33=9.The amount of parameters that must be memorized while employing 31 and 13 filters is 31+13=6. With asymmetric convolution, 33% reduction in the amount of parameters to be learned. Asymmetric convolution employed in Inception Module-B is depicted. It is suggested that Inception Module C be used to encourage high-dimensional representations. When considering the complete network, the total quantity of variables that can be learned is decreased by utilizing three different types of Inception Modules with various forms of factorized convolutions. The network can expand because the Inception Modules are less likely to over fit. The completely connected feature extraction and classification modules with the Softmax layer create pre-trained InceptionV3 model. The additional layer in InceptionV3 model is called the concatenation layer. Using this layer, characteristics from two different layers are concatenated. With feature extraction module, different features in an images are retrieved. Utilizing various convolutional layers, the feature extraction is carried out. The new dataset (OCT image dataset and Fundus image dataset) is used to retrain the classifier module. The challenging task is to train the classifier using the feature extraction module. When used for classifying new labels, this is not required. As a result, the model is trained using less computer power and in a shorter amount of time.

3.5.2 Model Inception ResnetV2

Training the InceptionResNetV2 convolutional neural network required thousands upon thousands of images from the ImageNet collection. Images of items like keyboards, mice, pens, and other creatures, this 164 layer network has image classification into 1000 distinct categories as illustrated in Figure 3.7. This network learns intricate Feature representations extracted from a diverse array of image types. Images with a maximum resolution of 299*299 pixels can be accepted by the network. Convolutions of various sizes make up the inception module, which allowing the network for process data at various spatial scales. Prior to the more costly 3x3 and 5x5 convolutions, 1x1 convolutions are employed for dimensionality reduction.

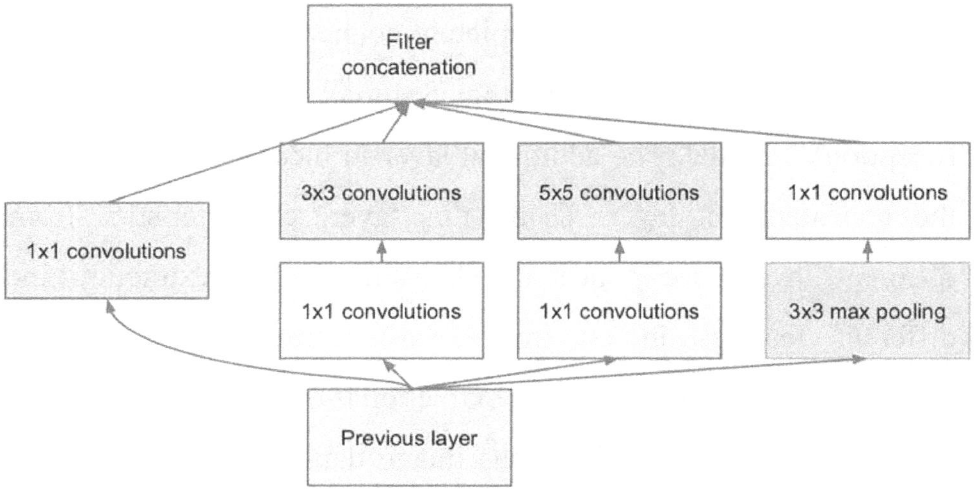

Figure 3.7 Inception block diagram

3.5.3 Model Xception

The profound deeply separable convolutions are used by CNNs, or the Xception architecture. Google researchers worked on developing it. They view CNN initialization modules as a transitional stage between standard and depth wise convolution. In this regard, a depth wise convolution is comparable to an Inception model with the maximum number of towers. Their groundbreaking deep CNN design, which takes its cues from Inception but substitutes depth-wise separable convolutions for Inception model, is made possible by this research.

3.6 MODEL RESNET50

Deep residual networks have convolutional, fully linked, pooled and activated layers layered on top of one another, just like deep NN. A simple network can be modified into a residual network by adding Identity links between the layers as shown in Figure 3.8. At the termination of residual block, the input represents curving trajectory that descends from identity connection.

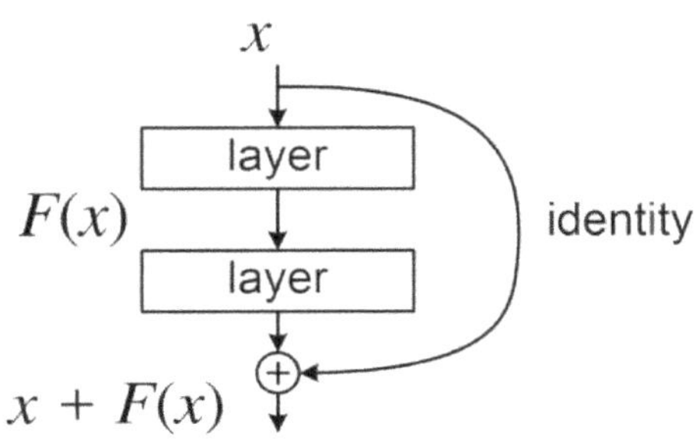

Figure 3.8 Deep residual network

Residual mapping or residual function refers to the difference between residual blocks of input and output. The value added to the input by block's last function is referred to as residual mapping. The residual mapping represents the highest degree of inaccuracy which can be incorporated into input in order to achieve intended result or resemble the end function. It is possible to see residual mapping.

3.6.1 ResNet50 Model Architecture

ResNet50 network receives an images with dimensions of 224 by 224 pixels and with 3 color channels. The initial convolution operation is performed by using kernel of size 7*7 in every ResNet network. The initial max-pooling operation is implemented by using kernel of size 3×3.

After performing these two operations, the network will begin at stage 1, the structure comprises three residual blocks, with each block including three layers. The convolution procedure over three levels of stage 1 block employs kernels of sizes 64, 64 and 128.

The bottleneck design is employed in deeper networks such as ResNet50, ResNet152 and similar architectures. Each residual function F consists of three stacked convolutional layers: one 1×1, one 3×3 and one 1×1. Dimension restoration is accomplished using the 1x1 convolution layers. Despite lower input/output size, the 3×3 layer remains a bottleneck. In figure 3.9, a FC layer of 1000 neurons for a 1000 class classification issue comes after the network's Average Pooling layer.

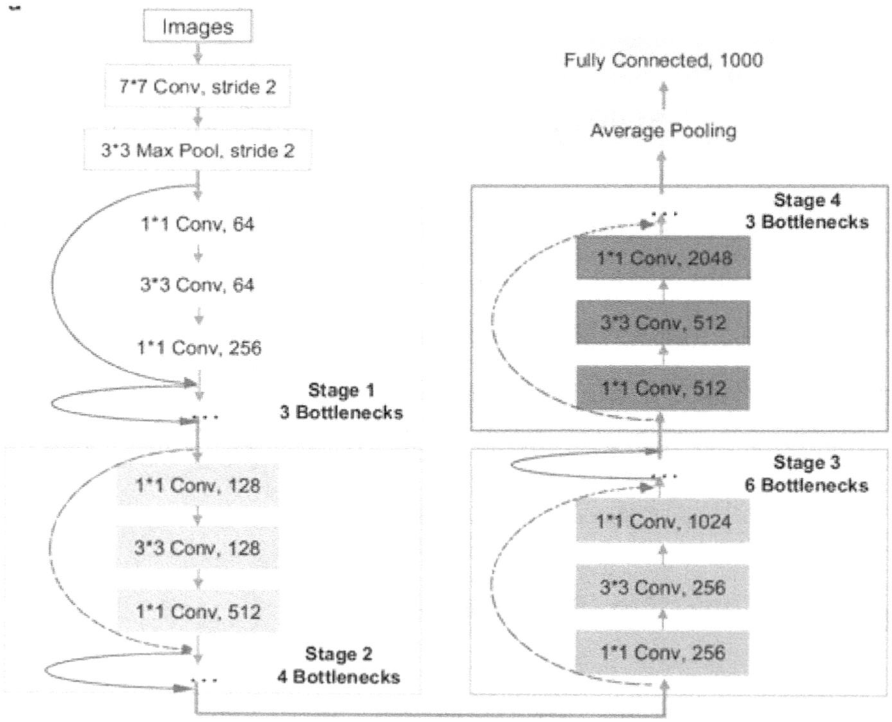

Figure 3.9 ResNet50 Model Architecture

3.7 DENSENET MODELS

An obvious progression of ResNet is DenseNet architecture. The Identity block is an essential part of ResNet50 design. Additive merging occurs between a previous and subsequent layer in ResNet50. The network must acquire residuals (errors, i.e., disparities between a former layer and current one) by adding additive merges. Instead of utilizing the summation, DenseNet concatenates the outputs from the preceding layers.

Recent research and development has demonstrated that convolutional networks can be trained to be shorter connections between layers make them considerably deeper, more precise and efficient, which are close to the input and output. In DenseNet, a sort of convolutional network, there exists a feed-forward link that connects each layer to every other layer. Figure 3.10 illustrates a CNN with L layers and L connections connecting these layers. Each layer is connected to the previous layer by a single connection. On the other hand, DenseNet has a total of L (L+1)/2 direct connections.

Each subsequent layer in the network is fed with feature-maps generated by all preceding layers. This layer provides all feature-map inputs for the layers that follow. Dense networks, which may also improve feature propagation, encourage the reuse of features and significantly reduce the number of parameters, which may be employed to address the issue of disappearing gradients.

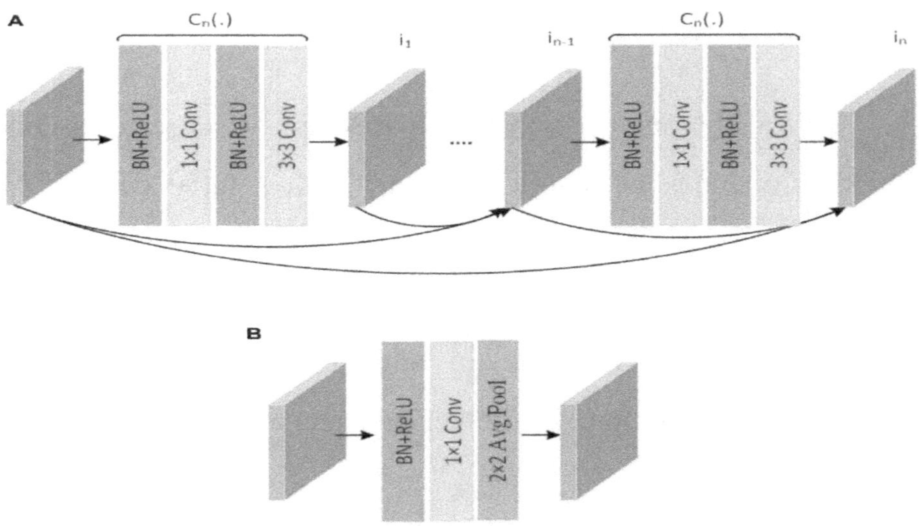

Figure 3.10 (A) DenseNet block and (B) Transition block

Dense connection pattern of DenseNets needs less parameters compared to typical convolutional networks. This is for redundant feature map relearning is not necessary in highly linked networks. One way to conceptualize traditional feed-forward architectures is as sequential transmission of state-containing algorithms from one layer to the next.

Each layer reads its current state from the layer below and passes it to the layer above, while also retaining data needed for future classification. ResNets are designed to explicitly preserve this information through additive identity transformations. Studies on various ResNet versions have shown that many layers contribute minimally to the final classification, allowing them to be removed during training. Currently, ResNets function similarly to unrolled recurrent neural networks, but with significantly more parameters since each layer has its own distinct weight.

The DenseNet architecture distinctly separates data that is added to the network from data that is retained. Each layer in DenseNet has only a few layers and produces twelve feature maps. A tiny fraction of these feature maps help to produce the collective knowledge output of networks. In final output layer of the classification system, all the feature maps in given network are considered before making a decision. DenseNets enhanced both network gradients and information flow, while also boosting parameter efficiency, making it easy to train. DenseNet layers possess direct access to gradients originating from original input signal as well as loss function, hence enabling the facilitation of deep supervision. This is particularly beneficial for training more complex network architectures. It was discovered that dense connections had a regularizing impact, reducing overfitting, especially in the tasks with smaller training sizes.

Feature maps that are learnt by different layers are integrated to improve efficiency and diversify the input for following layers. This will be one of the main differences between ResNets and DenseNets. Inception networks also combine attributes from several layers. However, as compared to Inception Networks, DenseNets are more user-friendly and efficient in reusing features. Every layer in DenseNets adds k distinct feature-maps to this state. The rate at which feature-maps expand is controlled and determined by the quantity of new data that each layer adds to overall state.

In DenseNets, each layer generates data that can be accessed from any part of the network, eliminating the need to duplicate new data across layers. Once a sufficient number of composite operations are performed, the output from one layer is connected to the next using standard feed-forward neural network connections, as illustrated in the DenseNet architecture. The composite function is composed of three elements: an activation function, batch normalization and a convolution process, commonly referred to as pooling layers. The following Equation 3.1 is used to represent the DenseNets composite operation.

$$x_l = H_l(x_{l-1}) \tag{3.1}$$

This behavior of composite operations, including the skip connection, was also expanded by ResNets. The ResNets' operation is represented by a combination of composite operations and skip connections. Equation 3.2 uses the two operations together to represent the two operations.

$$x_l = H_l(x_{l-1}) + x_{l-1} \tag{3.2}$$

DenseNets concatenate the layer's output and incoming feature maps, rather than adding them together.

3.8 BENEFITS OF CNN'S AND COMPARISON OF VARIOUS TECHNIQUES

1. Proficient at identifying patterns and discerning qualities or aspects in images, audio and video they are unaffected by scaling, rotation and translation.

2. Manual feature extraction may be avoided with full training.

3. CNN has excellent accuracy and is able to manage substantial volumes of data.

4. The effect of DIABETIC RETINOPATHY attained various accuracy levels, built on the several analysis of network model architecture.

5. This comparison has impacted in the proposed work to further enhance the accuracy w.r.t the dynamic DOT HEMORRHAGE (DH).

6. VGGNet is more accurate than other models along with having a greater number of parameters.

7. It takes approximately the same time to train an Alex Net as it does an Inception. With increased accuracy, ten times less memory is needed.

8. In this work, the research considers **VGG16 model architecture** to attain the enhanced accuracy using APTOS datasets.

The CNNs are categorized and presented in Table 3.1 according to the top-5 accuracy on the ImageNet dataset.

Table 3.1 Comparison of several CNN models with the DIARET dataset

MODEL	YEAR	PARAMETER	ACCURACY ON IMAGENET	ARCHITECTURE
Alex-net	2012	60M	84.70%	8 Convolution layers 3 FC layers
VGG-16	2014	138M	93%	16 Convolution layers 3 FC layers
Inception	2014	6.4M	90.27%	Wider-parallel kernels
Res-Net50	2015	25.6M	91.30%	50 Convolution layers with residual connections

3.9 SUMMARY

As the prevalence of Diabetic Retinopathy continues to increase globally on a daily basis, it is emerging as a leading cause of blindness. Reducing the blindness rate caused by DR requires early detection through accurate diagnosis. Today's DR screening demands more than ever for an automated system. The main techniques employed for this include DL, ML and pattern recognition & image classification. The most appropriate way to use when screening the DR for classification is to use deep learning techniques like CNN, as demonstrated by the results. Using fundus pictures for DR classification presents several significant challenges, some of which are listed below: i) Local minima and the CNN's vanishing gradient issue are brought on by back-propagation. ii) Accurately and comprehensively extracting characteristics from the fundus images. iii) Firstly, the main objective is to develop an automated system capable of DR identification.

Even if DR has been classified using a variety of DL techniques, there have been several issues that have emerged in CNN from different experimental approaches. Consequently, these points are attempted to be addressed by using ML techniques.

CHAPTER 4

DETECTION OF DIABETIC RETINAL DOT HEMORRHAGE USING DYNAMIC IMAGE COMPARISON WITH DEEP NEURAL NETWORKS

4.1 INTRODUCTION

This chapter provides background information on diabetic retinal DOT hemorrhages. Along with the methods for feature extraction of dynamic image analysis and the comparison which covers how to detect dot hemorrhages in diabetic retinopathy. It deals with the classification of retinal dot hemorrhages and image comparison of different stages with the classifiers are employed. It also provides the suggested architecture and algorithm of the classifiers for convolution neural network-based image comparison. It also examines the severity of stage classification, performance metrics, accuracy and outcomes of the experiments involving vision loss.

This chapter elucidates the behavior of a classification model in identifying diabetic retinopathy under different scenarios. By analyzing the model's behavior in respect to those parametric variables and their sorts, this work aims to produce a more diabetic retinopathy detection using a performative model. In order to classify diabetic retinopathy, a CNN model is created and various combinations of hyper-parameters are utilized. With a variety of assessment parameters, the shift in output values caused by the hyper-parameters is examined and assessed. The analysis demonstrates that the impact of diverse circumstances and model hyper-parameter values vary significantly for every unique combination.

DR has emerged as the most common form of diabetic eye disease in recent years. As diabetes advances, an increased amount of fluid and a small volume of blood flow infiltrate the eye through the damaged blood vessels of retina, potentially leading to the formation of particular retinal hemorrhages. A systemic condition or an uncontrolled ocular disorder may be indicated by retinal hemorrhages. Hemorrhages in the retina are an important ocular diagnostic indicator of a systemic vascular disease. Considering the hemorrhages' dimensions, depth and pattern, we can speculate about the possible underlying cause. To determine the source and to choose the apt course of action to prevent eyesight loss, some tools are required: a camera, detector, process analytical technology, foam analyzer and line photometric stereo imaging scan. To diagnose and treat retinal hemorrhages, a multidisciplinary team is mandatory. According to their severity stages, the retinal pictures in the current study are categorized as DH Severe, Mild, Moderate and No_DH. Figure 4.1 displays both the normal and dot hemorrhage retinal images.

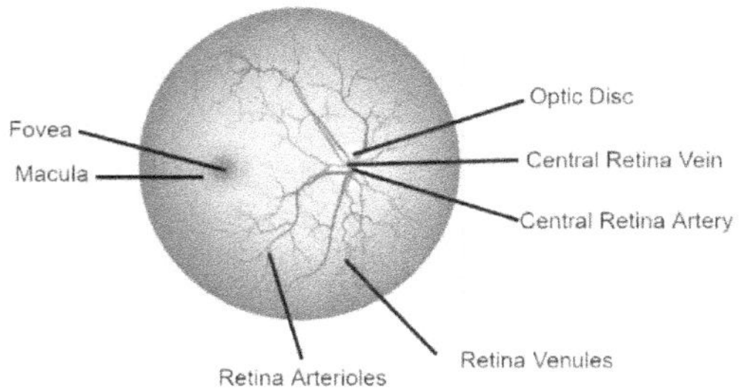

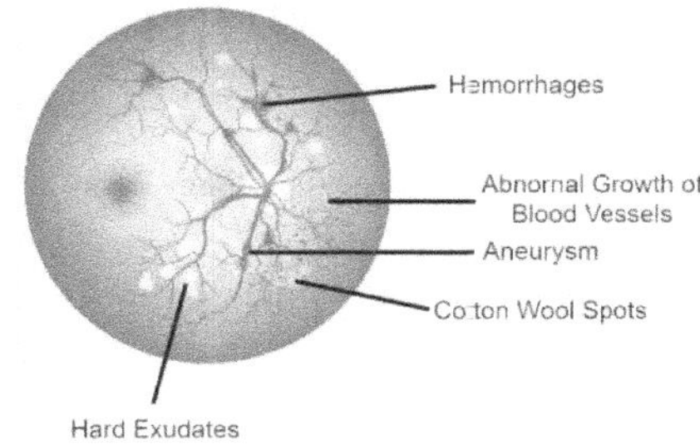

Figure 4.1(a) Healthy retina (b) Dot hemorrhage in the retina

A comprehensive overview of the significant research on detection of hemorrhages using retinal fundus images. An approach to supervised learning that uses splat feature classification to identify retinal fundus images in which hemorrhages is found. Using the MESSIDOR database, this method yields an operating characteristic curve for the receiver is 0.96 [63]. A technique for identifying lesions and vascular segments and demonstrating how shape changes during picture flooding that uses color retinal fundus images and dynamic form characteristics to detect hemorrhage and MAs.

Using MESSIDOR database, this approach produced a FROC score of 0.420 and a ROC curve of 0.899 [64]. A method of feature classification that uses retinal fundus images to identify the hemorrhage. Gaussian filters are used to the green channel outcome after features are extracted from the output of filter banks. The final collection of retrieved characteristics is then ascertained by applying the wrapper and filter method [65].

4.2 MOTIVATION

Based on the analysis of the various schemes, The DIARETDB1 dataset was found to have meager accuracy to detect the existence of DOT Hemorrhage in Diabetic Retinopathy. Hence this has motivated to opt for APTOS dataset to further detect the presence and enhance the accuracy of DR.

4.3 IMAGE COMPARISON METHOD USING DEEP CONVOLUTION NEURAL NETWORK

A diabetic patient needs routine eye exams to avoid getting hemorrhages of the retinal illness. If hemorrhages in diabetic retinopathy are treated early, vision loss can be prevented. Dot hemorrhages can be treated when they are first noticed because they do not have a major impact on the eye. Blindness may results from dot hemorrhages illness as it progresses. A diabetic patients needs to have regular eye screenings and exams. Each patient's manual screening requires a significant amount of time and money. Advanced medical image processing and comparison techniques allows automated diagnosis of DR's early hemorrhage signs, including blood vessel and hemorrhages spot.

The early diagnosis of these anomalies may aid in prompt and efficient treatment, shielding the eye from blindness. The majority of researchers made use of FA images or fundus color retinal images from the funduscopic taken with dilated pupils of the patients. Hemorrhages and blood vessels are identified individually and high contrast enhancement proposed classifiers are provided for identifying and rating abnormalities. The fundamental purpose of the current research is to identify dynamic dot hemorrhages from dynamic foam analyzer inline photometric stereo imaging and its contribution is to increase the early diagnosis's precision. Figure 4.2 displays the image anomalies, which include hemorrhages and blood vessels.

The color retinal dynamic images are pre-processed and transmitted to feature extraction. After pre-processing, features like hemorrhages are retrieved and the grading process is carried out. On several conditions, the intensity of hemorrhages has been graded. In order to determine how the chosen filter affects improving classification accuracy, this study used the CNN algorithm with the VGG16 learning architecture and the Gaussian Filter technique. This study also included other cases where different dataset treatments, either with or without the use of dynamic images, were paired with the VGG16 architecture. The classifiers that are taught to determine the normal (No_DR), mild, moderate, or severe of diabetic retinopathy.

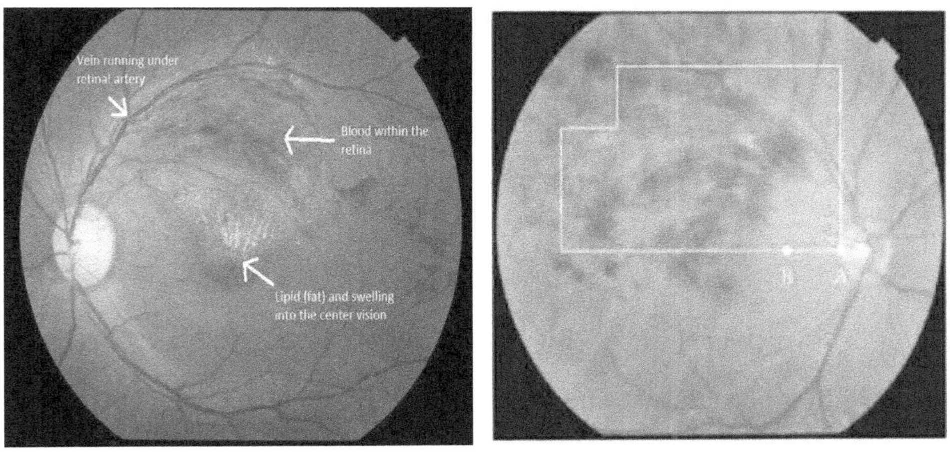

Figure 4.2 (a) Retinal blood vessels and (b) Hemorrhages

4.4 PROPOSED METHOD FOR DETECTING DOT HEMORRHAGES

We proposed a novel method for automatically detecting dot hemorrhages, it describes the process of microaneurysm production, which serves as an early sign of diabetic retinopathy in patients, as shown in Figure 4.3. Our approach offers the following contributions:

1. The edge (exo) details are enhanced using modified contrast enhancement (CLAHE) technique from input retinal fundus images.

2. Hemorrhages are detected using a distinct CNN design.

3. An upgraded VGG16 DL architecture extracts attributes from hemorrhages to extract features.

4. The best features are finally chosen utilizing the multiclass LR on entropy variance approach.

5. 3662 images for training and 1928 images for testing from APTOS databases are used to evaluate the proposed approach.

An ophthalmologist can diagnose hemorrhages faster with the suggested approach, which also guarantees consistent detection accuracy. In less time and at a reduced cost the suggested automated system produces precise results than the other methods. We suggest a unique hemorrhage detection method, which is further discussed in the next section, as a solution to the aforementioned issues.

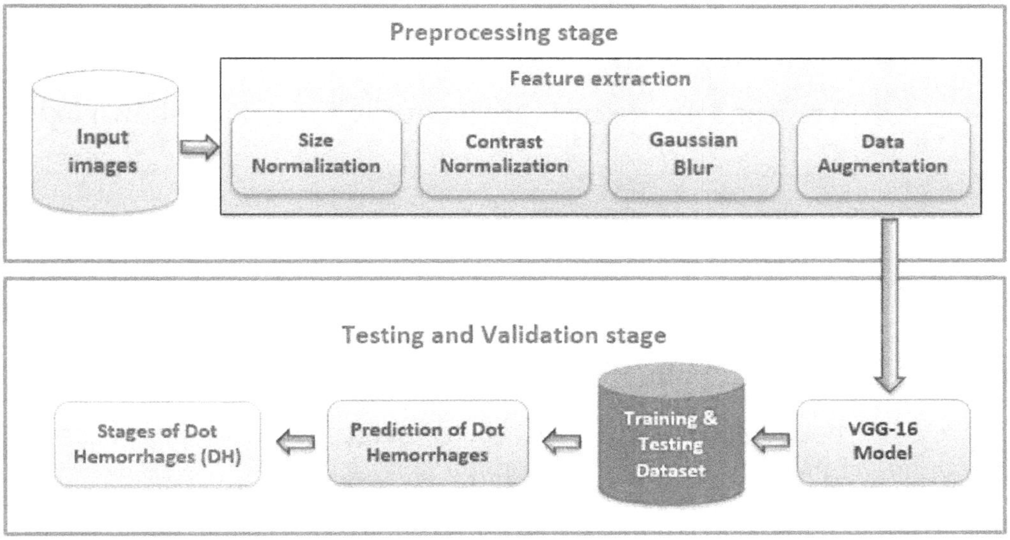

Figure 4.3 Proposed Block diagram for Dot Hemorrhage detection

4.4.1 Analyzing the APTOS Dataset

The total number of training images : 3662

The total number of testing images : 1928

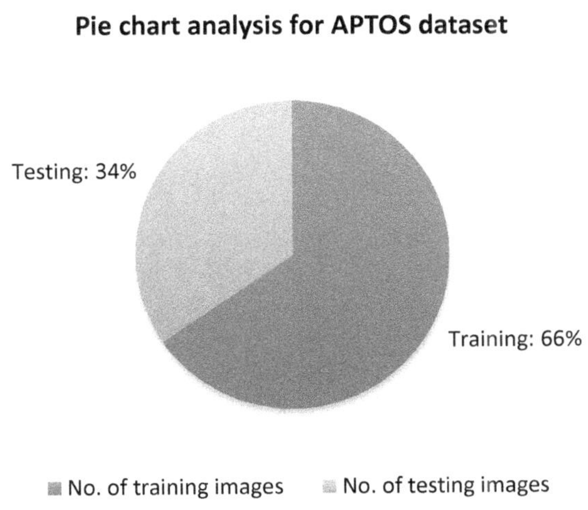

Figure 4.4 Size of training and testing dataset

Remarks:

- Train and test datasets are moderately sized are shown in Figure 4.4.
- The training set comprises three times more data compared to test set.
- Diabetic retinopathy severity has been assigned a stages between 0 and 4 on each images by the physicians. The challenge has five target classes and is multi-class.

The fundus images at each DR stage are shown in Figure 4.5. The second, third and fourth phases are referred as NPDR, while last stage is known as PDR.

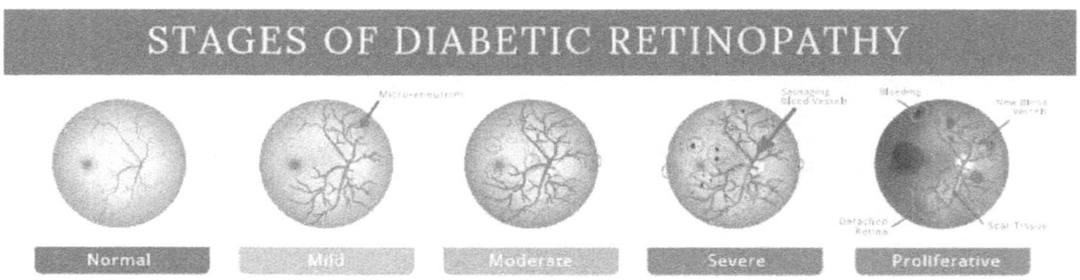

Figure 4.5 Different stages of DR image

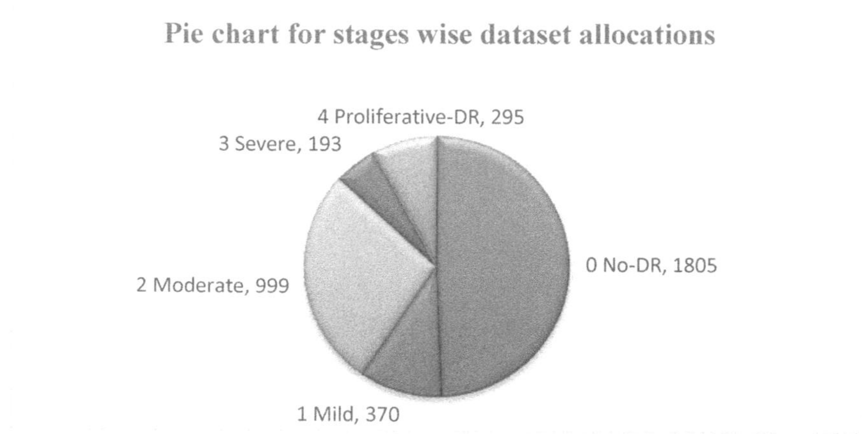

Figure 4.6 Pie chart for stage-wise dataset allocations

Remarks:

- In Figure 4.6, the number of images without DR is ten times higher than that of images with severe conditions.
- Class wise levels: 0 - No DR, 1 - Mild, 2 - Moderate 3 - Severe, 4 - Proliferative DR

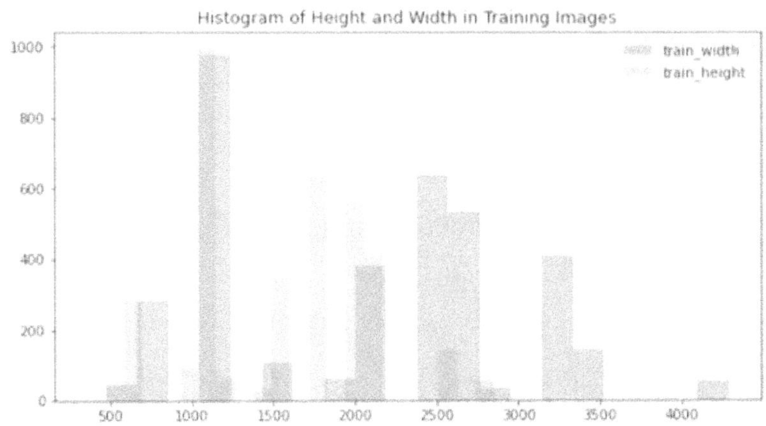

Figure 4.7 Histogram of height and width in training images

Figure 4.7 provides details about the testing and training in relation to height and width. Neither the training nor the test images have a fixed shape. To avoid compressing the informative pixels, we must resize all images to a sufficiently high standard resolution.

4.5 PRE-PROCESSING STAGES OF DYNAMIC IMAGES

Image identification and computer vision are two of the most widely used fields of advanced computation. RGB Color (Red, Green and Blue) channels are used to read and interpret the image. A × B × 3 indicates that the images contain A columns, B rows and three color channels. Given the high pixel density of most images, a fully connected neural network would need a large number of weights in its first hidden layer alone.

In Figure 4.8, the technique uses a set of dynamic images that have been properly pre-processed and applies traditional threshold level detection. Through pixel-by-pixel comparison with a reference picture, computers are able to identify and extract data from these images and help link the reference images to deformed ones. The computer analyzes each image section by section to compare them; these segments are referred to as features. Compared to matching full images, segment comparison greatly simplifies image detection and identification.

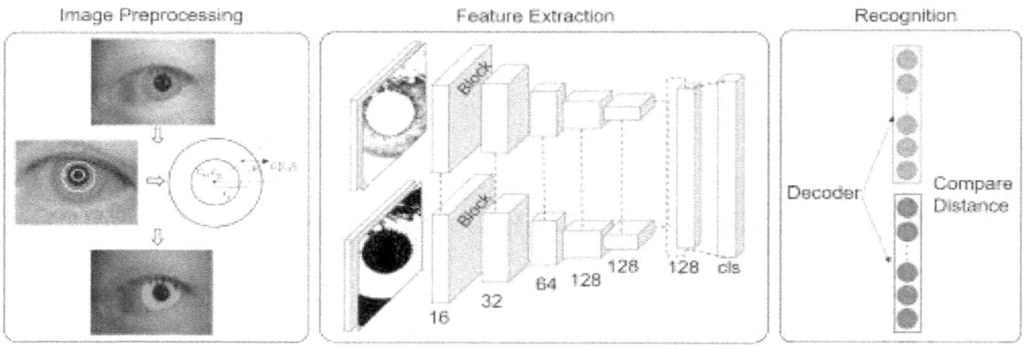

Figure 4.8 Dynamic image Pre-processing

4.6 NORMALIZATION IN IMAGE PREPROCESSING

In image processing, normalization alters the pixel intensity range. Applications include images with poor contrast induced by glare. Normalization can also be referred to as contrast or histogram stretching. Digital signal processing in other words dynamic range expansion is a data processing field.

The following assertions will consistently be accurate when using this normalization technique:

1. The dataset's lowest value will always have a normalized value of 0, or 0.

2. The dataset's highest value will always have a normalized value of 1, which is 1.

3. All other values in the dataset's normalized values will range from 0 to 1.

4.6.1 Image Resizing

The images sourced from APTOS databases and varying in size, are resized to a standard 224 x 224 pixels for further processing. After size normalization, an empirical selection is made for this size. Ensuring uniformity in image dimensions throughout the dataset is crucial for efficient analysis and training of models.

4.6.2 Image Contrast

Local Contrast Normalization (LCN) is a technique for non-linearly adjusting an image's contrast. LCN operates on local patches of the image on a per-pixel basis rather than doing global normalization throughout the entire image's range of values. To accomplish this, subtract the neighborhood mean from a specific pixel and divide the result by the range of pixel values. (Unit variance with zero mean, the Gaussian).

4.6.3 Gaussian Blur

A linear filter called a Gaussian filter, sometimes known as a Gaussian blur [55], is used to smooth out images and minimize the noise. Carl Gauss is used in this windowed filter as its honorary name. The weighted average is calculated using the Gaussian distribution often referred to as the bell-function. One and two dimensional spatial situations can make use of it. The filter's cut-off frequency (Fc) can be defined as by dividing sample rate (Fs) by the standard deviation (σ). The relationships are given in the following Equations 4.1 and 4.2.

$$Fc = Fs/\sigma \tag{4.1}$$

The equation gives the 1D Gaussian filter.

$$G(x) = \frac{1}{\sqrt{2\pi\sigma^2}} e^{-\frac{x^2}{2\sigma^2}} \tag{4.2}$$

Where σ represents the distribution's standard deviation. We assume that the mean of distribution is zero at $\sigma = 0$, $x = 0$. The distribution is illustrated below: When working with two-dimensional images, the distribution generates a surface with outlines depicted as Gaussian-distributed concentric circles radiating outward from the center. A convolution matrix are generated from distributed values and used on original image. The neighborhood of each pixel is averaged in weight and this average is used to determine the pixel's new value. The initial value of pixels is assigned the most importance and this decreases as the distance between them increases, their weights decrease. The following characteristics of Gaussian functions make them helpful in image processing.

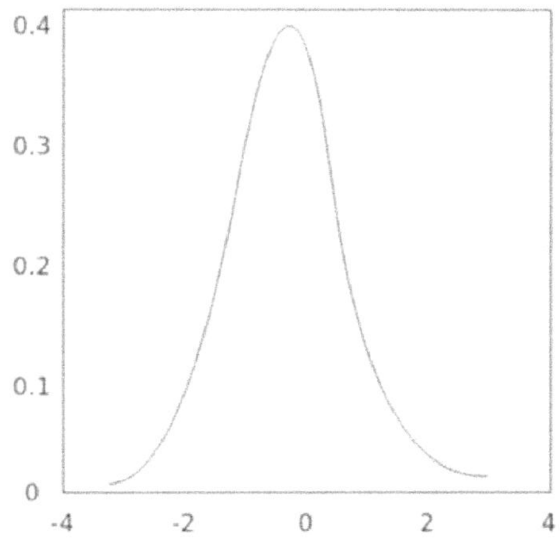

Figure 4.9 Gaussian Characteristics

- Gaussian functions exhibit rotational symmetry in two dimensions. Rotationally symmetric means that the filter will produce the same amount of smoothing in all directions. A Gaussian filter won't influence the direction of subsequent edge detection because it is rotationally symmetric.

- The frequency spectrum of a Gaussian's Fourier transform only has one lobe shown in the Figure 4.9. High frequency noise frequently distorts images and the desirable aspect of the image will be spread across both the low and high frequency spectra. Since a Gaussian's Fourier transform only has one lobe, the smoothed image won't be tainted by contributions from undesirable high frequency signals while the majority of the favorable signal features will still be there.

- A variance controls the smoothing's level of intensity. A wider Gaussian filter and more smoothing are suggested by more variance.

- Gaussian functions in two dimensions can be separated. This characteristic indicates that relatively efficient implementation of massive Gaussian filters is possible. By first transforming the image into a one-dimensional Gaussian and then using the same one-dimensional filter with an orientation orthogonal to the Gaussian used in the first stage, one can conduct a two-dimensional Gaussian convolution.

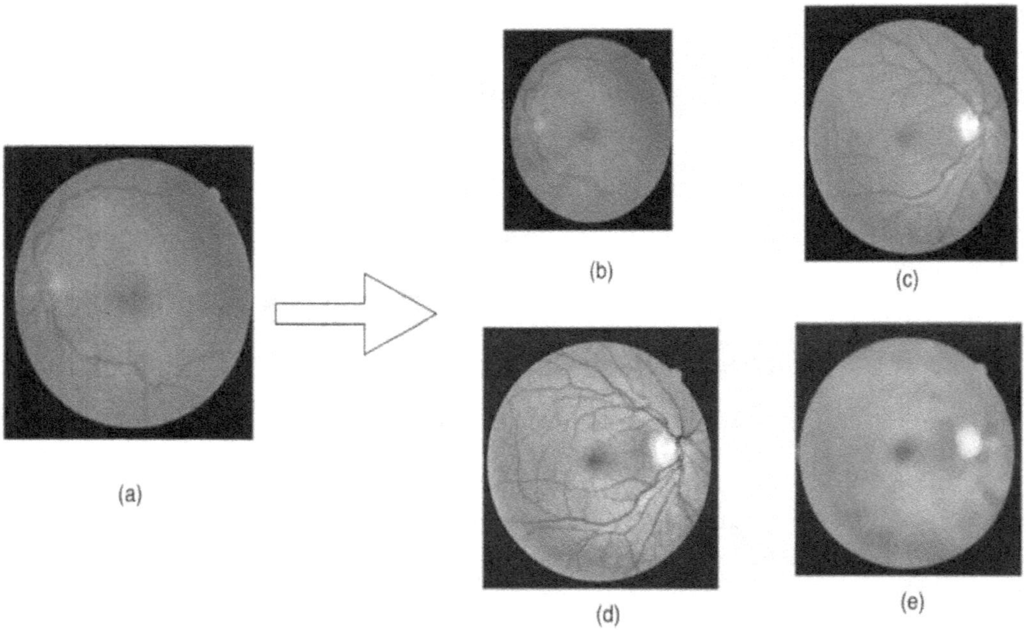

Figure 4.10 (a) Input image (b) Image resizing, (c) Image with Gaussian blur (d) Image after noise has been eliminated and (e) Final pre-processed image

4.6.4 Image after Noise Elimination

The image undergoes additional noise reduction. This step typically involves filtering techniques to remove remaining noise and artifacts, enhancing the clarity of important features in the image.

4.6.5 Final Pre-Processed Image

The image after all preprocessing steps is the final version used for analysis or model training. It is a cleaned, standardized and noise-free representation of the original image, ready for further processing or classification as shown in Figure 4.10.

4.7 EXTRACTION OF FEATURES

Feature selection, which picks a portion of a given measurement as features, is a specific instance of feature extraction. The selected characteristics must possess the capability to differentiate between objects belonging to different classes. The process of selecting features is understandable as mapping from underlying n-dimensional space into lower dimensional space. Selecting a sufficient number of characteristics to be included in the classification while maintaining the accuracy of the classification at a tolerable level is the fundamental aim of feature selection.

Feature extraction is essential since the extracted features will be used to carry out the ultimate classification and train the Neural Network. APTOS database is employed to classify images as normal or abnormal by evaluating diameter, highest intensity and lowest intensity of the optic disc, blood vessels and areas that have been affected by injury. Following characteristic features are added: variance, entropy, area, mean and perimeter.

Using the Standard Diabetic Retinopathy Database, the following metrics were retrieved for the classification of dot hemorrhage from aberrant retinal pictures: mean, variance, cross correlation, autocorrelation, covariance, area, perimeter, entropy and minimum and maximum intensities.

More than 72 characteristics were acquired for dividing exudates into soft and hard classification. In APTOS Database, features including variance, cross correlation and covariance are utilized to classify dot hemorrhage. Comparable features are implemented for the Database.

4.8 EXTRACTION OF OPTIC DISC, DETECTION OF BLOOD VESSEL AND SEGMENTATION OF DAMAGE AREA

Following segmentation, feature extraction are performed. This stage is crucial because the neural network will be trained and retrieved features will be used for classification. Some of the extracted features are area, diameter, perimeter, mean, variance, entropy, maximum and minimum intensity of the image's R, G and B components are determined individually. Every feature is combined to form the feature vector.

4.8.1 Features of Optical Disks

The number of pixels in the segment's boundary is used to compute the perimeter. Assume, $P_1, P_2, \dots, P_N, \dots P_M$ are the pixels in the segment, where N is the no. of pixels in the segment's boundary region, A is the area and P is the perimeter. The entropy of pixels is computed using the following Equation 4.3:

$$e = -\sum_i p_i \log_2 p_i \qquad (4.3)$$

p_i, the difference in probability between two neighboring pixels is denoted as i and log2 represents base-2 logarithms.

Maximum intensity refers to the highest pixel intensity within segment, while minimum intensity denotes the lowest intensity in segment. If the pixel segment's $P_1, P_{2...,} P_M$ have intensity as $I_1, I_2 ..., I_M$, then maximum Intensity is equal to maximum$(1_1, 1_2, ..., 1_M)$.

4.8.2 Area of Damage Features

Damage area segmentation yields the area and damage values. The area is defined as the total number of pixels within section, as previously mentioned. The damage area is determined as either 1 or 0. If any damage areas are identified, the retinal image input exhibits damage, with a region damage value of one; otherwise, it is zero. In this instance, Equation 4.4 uses a D_a to represent the area damage value,

$$D_a = \begin{cases} 1, \text{If any area of damage is detected} \\ 0, \text{if no area of damage is detected} \end{cases} \tag{4.4}$$

4.8.3 Blood Vessel Characteristics

Mean, diameter and variance are taken from the blood vessel segmentation. The Equation 4.5 gives the average intensities of an image.

$$\bar{X} = \sum_{i=1}^{N} \frac{x_i}{n} \tag{4.5}$$

where 'n' is the no. of pixels in image and x_i is image's pixel intensity. The following Equation 4.6 may be used to calculate the variance of intensity of image pixels,

$$M_{nen} = \sum_x \sum_y x^n y^n I(x,y) \tag{4.6}$$

4.9 EXTRACTION OF FEATURE FROM EXUDATES

After the exudates have been segmented, two additional segments namely optical disc and blood vessels are obtained for the purpose of feature extraction. The NN will undergo training and then execute the final classification using extracted features, feature extraction is crucial. Mean, perimeter, variance, entropy, area, maximum intensity, minimum intensity, cross correlation, auto correlation and co-variance are amongst the features collected. The optic disc, blood vessels and injury area are all estimated for three segmented regions, the improved FCM is then fed into a NN classifier to recognize soft and hard exudates. The attributes are:

4.9.1 Automatic Correlation

The two images autocorrelation coefficient is

$$r = \frac{\sum_i (x_i-\bar{x})(y_i-\bar{y})}{\sqrt{(x_i-\bar{x})^2\sqrt{(y_i-\bar{y})^2}}} \tag{4.7}$$

where x and y are the mean intensities of pixels, and x_i and y_i are the intensities of the corresponding pixels $\bar{x}$ and $\bar{y}$

4.9.2 The Cross-correlation

The cross correlation formula for the image I(x, y) is given by Equations 4.8.

$$I(x,y) = \sum h[x,y]b[x+i,y+i],\ \mathrm{i} = 1,\ldots,\mathrm{N_b}, \mathrm{j} = 1,\ldots,\mathrm{M_b} \quad (4.8)$$

where,

$$i = -\frac{(N_h-1)}{2},\ldots\frac{(N_h-1)}{2}$$
$$j = -\frac{(M_h-1)}{2},\ldots\frac{(M_h-1)}{2}$$

The variables Mb and Nb represent the dimensions of a template, which is a smaller image extracted from a bigger image. Similarly, Mh and Nh represent the dimensions of the image.

4.9.3 Co-variance

The segmented region's co-variation is given by Equation 4.9.

$$R_{iy}^2 = \frac{\sum_{i=1}^{n}(x_i-\bar{x})(y_i-\bar{y})}{n-1} \quad (4.9)$$

where,

R_{yj}^2- Sample covariance of variables x and y

x_i - Variable x values from i to n

$\bar{x}$ – The sample mean of variable x

y_i - Variable y values range from i to n

$\bar{y}$ - The sample mean of the variable y

n - sample size

4.10 NOISY IMAGE SYNTHESIS ADVANCED GAUSSIAN NOISE

The fundus image is overlaid with additive Gaussian noise to evaluate how sensitive the trained model is to noise when used for classification or picture captioning (mean = 1, variance = 0.002, 0.004). The original image is overlaid with additive Gaussian noise with mean equal to 1 and variance equal to 0.002, 0.004 in order to produce noisy images of retinal fundus. The size of an image that was read from the source site is verified. If the size is appropriate, a Gaussian noisy image with the same form as unique fundus images are generated. The original fundus image is combined with Gaussian noise after the size is modified.

When these steps are used, noisy Fundus images with Gaussian noise will be produced. By utilizing various variance values for the additive Gaussian noise, the noise's volume or intensity can be modified. The primary purpose of this image pre-processing is to define how much noise the model can accept before incorrectly classifying or captioning the images. To evaluate the model's vulnerability, Gaussian noise has two separate standard deviation (SD) values (0.002 and 0.004) is blended with OCT pictures to produce a noised image with varying strengths. To evaluate the model's efficacy in mitigating noise, the retinal fundus images are combined with GN and two additional sets of various SD values, equivalent to 0.01 and 0.02.

4.11 LIMITATIONS OF TRADITIONALLY USED METHODS FOR FEATURE EXTRACTION

Earlier, advancements in computer vision relied on manually created characteristics. On the other side, feature engineering is difficult, time-consuming and needs a professional expertise of the subject area. The amount of information that can be extracted from a picture by hand-engineered features like the Histogram of Oriented Gradients (HOG), Speeded-up Robust Feature (SURF) and Scale Invariant Feature Transform (SIFT) similar methods is also a challenge. The majority of computer vision applications, such as image categorization and object recognition, do not necessitate the use of first-order image derivatives.

Additionally, the application regularly decides which features are selected. To put it more precisely, these traits make it challenging to learn from previous experiences or representations (transfer learning). Furthermore, human complexity limitations on hand-engineered features restrict their design. Automatic feature learning systems, such as deep neural networks, can alleviate all concerns.

4.12 PROPOSED METHOD SIMULATION PROCESS

The proposed method consists of 5 phases:

1. Extraction of Green channel,
2. Contrast enhancement,
3. Segmentation based on CNN,
4. Training model,
5. Feature extraction using deep learning

1. Extraction of Green Channels:

Due of the intrinsically poor contrast of retinal fundus images, it is imperative to improve the contrast. To detect the ROI, color input images are converted to green channel in Figure 4.11 because it provides highest contrast between exudates, blood vessels, hemorrhages and optic disc. White lesions appear bright, while red lesions appear dark as a result. It is necessary to divide retinal fundus images into three channels.

2. Contrast Enhancement

One of the primary pre-processing stages in diagnostic procedures is contrast enhancement. The source retinal fundus images lack contrast because of insufficient lighting. For enhancing the low contrast images, the histogram equalization technique seems to be a more practical approach.

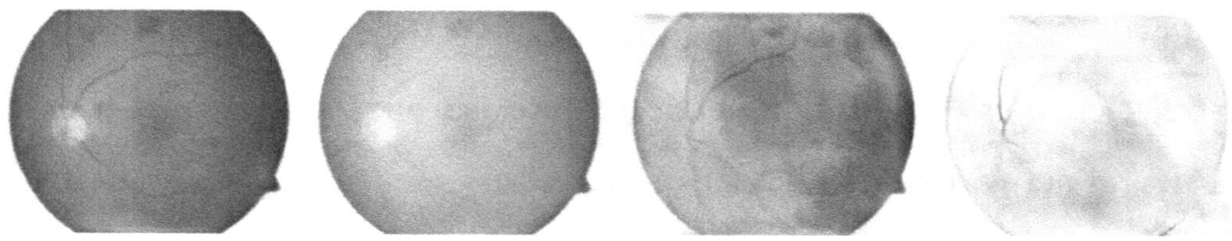

(a) (b) (c) (d)

Figure 4.11 RGB channel extraction from a colorful image (a) Original input image (b) R channel, (c) B channel and (d) G channel

An enhanced version of CLAHE is applied to improve contrast while maintaining the input images with middling brightness. CLAHE impact on small sections of image, known as tiles. The contrast limited histogram for the non-overlapping region was calculated using Equation (4.10) as follows:

$$Iavge = \frac{Nx*Ny}{Ng} \tag{4.10}$$

where Iavge, the average pixel number, Ng denotes the non-overlapping related region gray levels and Nx and Ny represent the number of pixels in x and y dimensions respectively.

Equation (4.11) computes the intensity values using Rayleigh transform.

$$I_y = I_{min} + \sqrt{2\alpha^2 ln\left(\frac{1}{1 - P_{in}}\right) I_{step}} \tag{4.11}$$

Figure 4.12 displays an increase in contrast through the 'G' channel, also demonstrate how the gradients are significantly improved after using our modified contrast enhancement technique.

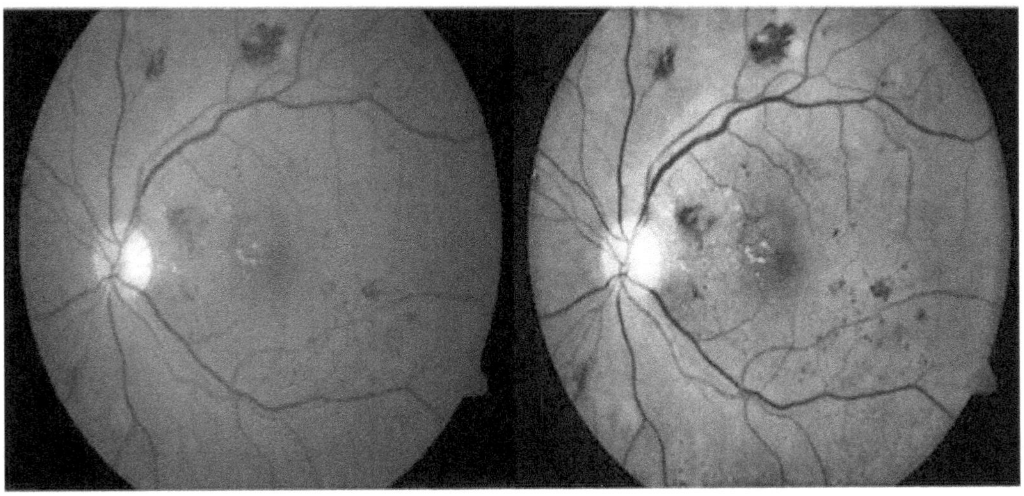

(a) (b)

Figure 4.12 The contrast-enhanced retinal fundus images a) Extraction of Green channel, b) Final contrast enhanced output image.

3. VGG-16 Detection

In CGG-16, thirteen convolutional layers and three completely FC layers make up its sixteen layers, which are responsible for its depth. Layers with increasing depth in max-pooling are stacked on top of a stack of convolutional layers in the architecture model. Efficient and precise predictions are generated by the model because to its ability to learn intricate hierarchical representations of visual data.

RGB-channeled images with a fixed 224*224 size are part of the ImageNet collection. Thus, a tensor of (224, 224, 3) represents our input. Following the processing of the input image, this model produces a vector that is divided into five stages: normal, mild, moderate, severe and advanced severe. This vector is the categorization probability for the corresponding class. The sum of these probabilities is guaranteed to equal one by applying the softmax function.

The VGG-16 architecture is outlined as:

1. Input Layer dimensions: (224, 224, 3)
2. Convolutional Layers: 64 filters with the same padding and 3x3 filters
    a. A pair of sequential convolutional layers with a 3x3 filter size and 64 filters each.
    b. To preserve spatial dimensions, the same padding is used.
3. (2×2, stride 2) Max Pooling Layer

4. Convolutional Layers: 128 filters, 3x3 filters and the same amount of padding

   a. Two consecutive layers of convolution, each with a 3x3 filter size and 128 filters.

5. (2×2, stride 2) Max Pooling Layer

6. Convolutional Layers: 256 filters, 3x3 filters, with identical padding

7. Convolutional Layers: 512 filters, 3x3 filters and the same amount of padding

8. (2×2, stride 2) Max Pooling Layer

9. Max Pooling with a stack of Convolutional Layers

   a. Following the prior stack, there are two further convolutional layers.

   b. Filter dimensions: 3 x 3.

10. Flattening: Create a vector with a size of 25088 by flattening the output feature map (7x7x512).

11. Fully Connected Layers (FC Layers)

    a. 3 fully connected layers that are activated by LReLU.

    b. 1st layer: Input size: 25088 and output size: 4096.

c. 2nd layer: input and output size: 4096.

d. 3rd layer: Input size: 4096 and output size: 1000.

e. For classification, Softmax activation is applied third FC layer's output.

An important factor in neural network models is learning rate. It is a hyper-parameter controlling the neural network model's learning rate [58]. Reducing the loss function of the network by scaling the weight's size is the primary purpose of learning rate. With each cycle, the weight is gradually changed to map the necessary values. These parameters are all necessary components of every CNN. Understanding their behavior with respect to any network, model, or data is necessary. To put it simply, learning or training is often carried out by changing weights that connect the input and output. Stochastic Gradient Descent (SGD), an empirical optimization methodology, is used to compute these updated weights analytically [59].

i. Full Convolution ensures valid input values by using the largest possible padding for input feature maps, ensuring convolutions at the corners have at least one acceptable value.

ii. The network learns non-linear mappings after convolutional and fully connected layers, with various activation functions for input t used in real-time applications.

4.13 EXPERIMENTATION RESULT ANALYSIS

Training Models

The evaluation criteria used in the trial are detailed below. The subsequent section will cover the analysis of outcomes, which is conducted in a step-by-step manner as outlined.

Phase 1: The model's number of iterations is analyzed during phase-1. The combinations chosen for each pooling are shown in the following tables, together with the accuracy levels that are tested across a range of iterations. Table 4.1 displays the various accuracy values for max pooling with different parameters. In accordance, min pooling, average pooling and maxmin pooling are displayed in Tables 4.2, 4.3 and 4.4.

Various learning rates, pooling layers, activation functions and optimization factors are explored within experimental setting, as previously mentioned. The model uses four activation functions: LReLu, ReLU, sigmoid and tanh. Its accuracy changes with parameter values and type of functions. Accuracy is not constant and may fluctuate with learning rate or iteration. Combinations are tested with an increase in iteration and the highest-performing combination is chosen for further testing with an increased epoch.

The tanh function is more suitable for average pooling, while the LReLu activation function performs well with min pooling. Their effectiveness differs with other pooling techniques. For this model and dataset, the AdaDelta optimizer excels in max pooling, whereas the Adam optimizer delivers improved results with maxmin and min pooling. The tables clearly demonstrate the performance of various parameters and conditions in this specific scenario.

Table 4.1 Phase 1 selective combinations for Max pooling

Pooling	Activation	Optimizer	Learning Rate	Iterations	Accuracy
MAX POOLING	ReLU	Adadelta	0.1	50	0.73
	LReLU	Adadelta	0.1	50	0.71
	LReLU	Adam	0.0001	75	0.751
	Tanh	Adadelta	0.01	75	0.72

Table 4.2 Phase 1 selective combinations for Min pooling

Pooling	Activation	Optimizer	Learning Rate	Iterations	Accuracy
MIN POOLING	ReLU	Adadelta	0.0001	25	0.761
	LReLU	Adadelta	0.1	50	0.724
	LReLU	ADAM	0.0001	50	0.724
	LReLU	ADAM	0.0001	100	0.715

Table 4.3 Phase 1 selective combinations for Average pooling

Pooling	Activation	Optimizer	Learning Rate	Iterations	Accuracy
AVERAGE POOLING	LReLU	ADAM	0.01	50	0.734
	Tanh	Adadelta	0.01	25	0.71
	Tanh	SGD	0.01	50	0.71
	Tanh	ADAM	0.0001	75	0.754

Table 4.4 Phase 1 selective combinations for Maxmin pooling

Pooling	Activation	Optimizer	Learning Rate	Iterations	Accuracy
MAXMIN POOLING	LReLU	ADAM	0.001	50	0.712
	Tanh	ADAM	0.0001	25	0.83

Phase 2: The aforementioned combinations are taken into consideration once more, this time with a 1500 iteration, and the results are examined. The accuracy determined using 1500 iterations against fewer than 100 iterations is contrasted in Tables 4.5, 4.6, 4.7 and 4.8 display the findings for various pooling like max, min, average and maxmin.

It is evident that certain accuracy values rise as the number of iterations increases, but other accuracy values drop because they may become stuck in local minima. Just a small percentage of these, denoted in bold text, improve accuracy with more iterations. Additionally, those combinational conditions for precision indicated are taken for exploration with a higher value of iteration.

Table 4.5 Phase 2 selective combinations for Max pooling

Pooling	Activation	Optimizer	Learning Rate	Accuracy (at ≤ 100)	Accuracy (at 1500 iteration)
MAX POOLING	ReLU	Adadelta	0.1	0.73	0.686
	LReLU	Adadelta	0.1	0.715	0.845
	LReLU	ADAM	0.0001	0.735	0.617
	Tanh	Adadelta	0.1	0.721	0.568

Table 4.6 Phase 2 selective combinations for Min pooling

Pooling	Activation	Optimizer	Learning Rate	Accuracy (at ≤ 100)	Accuracy (at 1500 iteration)
MIN POOLING	ReLU	ADAM	0.0001	0.754	0.569
	LReLU	Adadelta	0.1	0.735	0.569
	LReLU	ADAM	0.0001	0.735	0.637
	LReLU	ADAM	0.0001	0.715	0.568

Table 4.7 Phase 2 selective combinations for Average pooling

Pooling	Activation	Optimizer	Learning Rate	Accuracy (at ≤ 100)	Accuracy (at 1500 iteration)
AVERAGE POOLING	LReLU	ADAM	0.01	0.765	0.637
	Tanh	Adadelta	0.01	0.71	0.864
	Tanh	SGD	0.01	0.71	0.637
	Tanh	ADAM	0.0001	0.763	0.617

Table 4.8 Phase 2 selective combinations for Maxmin pooling

Pooling	Activation	Optimizer	Learning Rate	Accuracy (at ≤ 100)	Accuracy (1500 iteration)
MAXMIN POOLING	Tanh	ADAM	0.001	0.72	0.687
	LReLU	ADAM	0.0001	0.803	0.864

Phase 3: Three pooling technique combinations that are effective for this model and dataset are chosen here: max pooling, average pooling and maxmin pooling. Additionally, these combinations, which are listed in Table 4.9, can be applied in combination with hybridization or optimization methods to produce a more appropriate model with greater accuracy values.

In this experiment, two kinds of diabetic retinopathy are considered: normal and DR. A more thorough analysis looks at the five class DR problem, which consists of a normal stage and the remaining four stages are mild, moderate, severe and proliferative DR classes. This exam will help us to endeavors to more thoroughly classify DR.

Table 4.9 Phase 3 selective combination and their accuracy

Pooling	Activation	Optimizer	Learning Rate	Accuracy (at ≤ 100)	Accuracy (at 1500 iteration)
Average Pooling	**Tanh**	**Adadelta**	**0.01**	**0.71**	**0.864**
Maxmin Pooling	**LReLU**	**ADAM**	**0.0001**	**0.803**	**0.864**
Max Pooling	**LReLU**	**Adadelta**	**0.1**	**0.715**	**0.845**

4.14 MAJOR FINDINGS AND DISCUSSIONS

- Compared to the other pooling types used in this situation, maxmin pooling produces a noticeably superior result. High-quality pixels are generated during both the training as well as in testing phases for classification by pooling process combining the maximum and minimum pixel values.

- LReLu function transform's some negative values to zero, outperforms alternative activation functions, a good accuracy results.

- In this experiment, for CNN image classification, LReLu turned out to be the most efficient activation function; tanh function and ReLU also perform well in certain combinations.

- The study found that Adam and Adadelta optimizers provide over 50% good accuracy values in CNN cases, with Adadelta achieving less than 40% in combinational cases, and lower learning rates yield superior results in half cases.

- In conclusion, the Adam and Adadelta optimizers outperform the SGD optimizer for images in CNNs.

- In this experimental research on CNNs, smaller learning rates, such as 0.0001 and 0.001, produce better outcomes in half of the phase analyses.

For Hemorrhage detection, a CNN-based system is suggested. Input to the subsequent layers is supplied in the form of various corrections and this architecture works with 3D images to calculate features. Equation (4.12) gives the expression for the convolutional layer as:

$$\xi_i^q = I_i\left[\sum_{m=1}^{\kappa-1} \chi_i^{m,n} \times \xi_{i-1}^q + \vartheta_i^q\right] \tag{4.12}$$

LReLu activation function is utilized after the convolutional layer to expedite the training process. For every positive attribute, this function returns its identity, while for every negative attribute, it returns a zero. A more intricate image model is given by the following equation in Equation (4.13) and will be utilized subsequently to more accurately ascertain the nature of the pixel.

$$\zeta_{i-1} = \zeta_{i-1}^{1}, \zeta_{i-1}^{2}, \zeta_{i-1}^{3}, \ldots, \zeta_{i-1}^{K-1} \tag{4.13}$$

Furthermore, Equation (4.14) provides a mathematical computation of the overfitting problem, which is eliminated with the assistance of this function.

$$T = \max(0, \xi) \tag{4.14}$$

Our proposed method incorporates two max pooling layers to reduce the feature extents (Figure 4.13) and eliminate unnecessary spatial information.

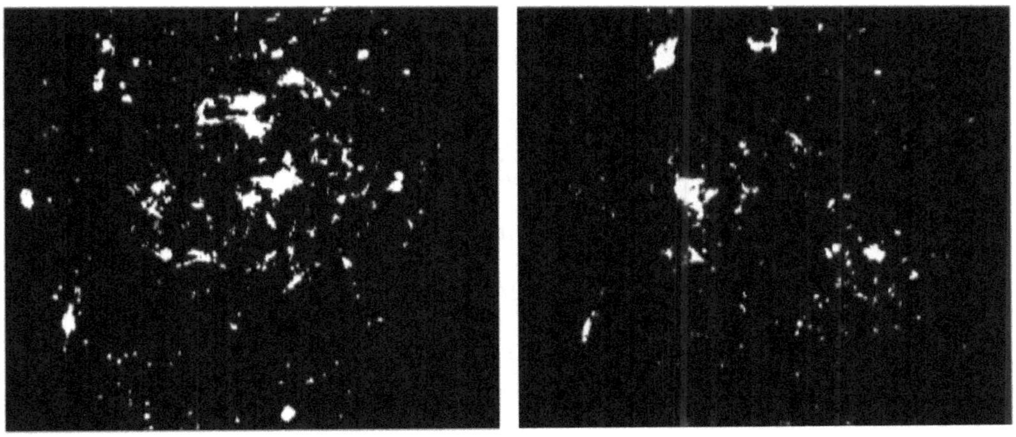

Figure 4.13 Proposed segmentation results

In Figure 4.14, hemorrhages are categorized using the cross-entropy function by incorporating a pixel label classification layer, as described in Equation 4.15.

$$\psi(\xi, Q) = -\frac{1}{V}\sum_{i=1}^{V} ln(R_Q) \quad (4.15)$$

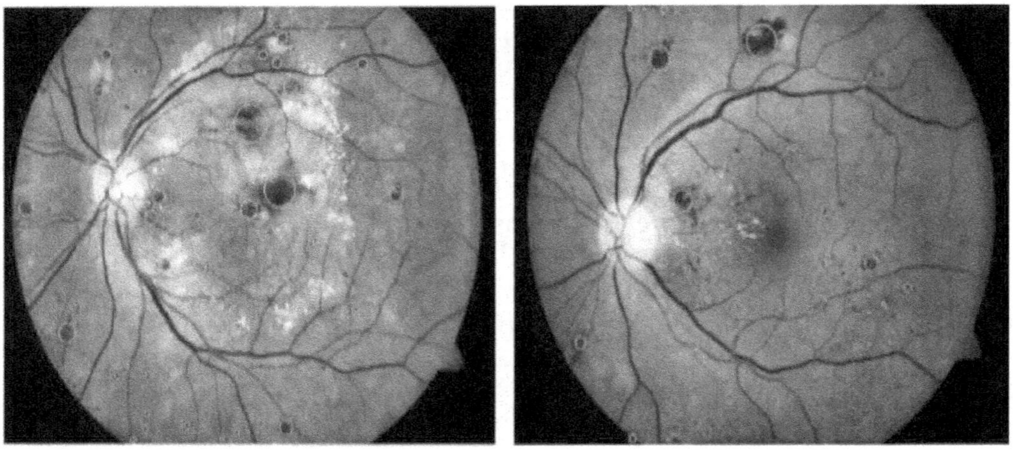

Figure 4.14 Hemorrhages Extraction output

4.15 PERFORMANCE ASSESSMENT

To evaluate the precision and proficiency of the algorithm, several alternative ways are proposed with the above suggested strategy. An Intel(R) Core(TM) i5 9750H 2.6GHz with 8GB RAM is used for the experiments. Model development and experimentation are carried out using Tensor Flow v1.12. Using images from the APTOS dataset, we evaluated how well our proposed algorithm detected hemorrhages. This experiment made use of 3662 color fundus images in total.

The testing dataset was divided into two groups: DR images and healthy images. These groups were determined by ophthalmologists with expertise in the provided datasets, who divided the 3662 images that showed 1857 hemorrhages images and 1805 healthy images. The total training images

4.16 METRICS TO EVALUATE THE CLASSIFICATION PHASE

The evaluation process involves applying the four quadrants of a confusion matrix to the following matrices:

- TP-True Positive : Positive class is correctly predicted.
- TN-True Negative : Negative class is correctly predicted.
- FP-False Positive : Positive class incorrectly predicted.
- FN-False Negative : Negative class incorrectly predicted.

Accuracy: In Equation 4.16, defines accuracy as the efficacy of a classifier in accurately classifying all data. The total no. of class levels is N.

$$Accuracy = (TP+TN) / \mathrm{N} \tag{4.16}$$

4.17 SUMMARY OF EXPERIMENTAL EVALUATION

The proposed method is carried out utilizing indicators like Accuracy. Using APTOS datasets, 3662 retinal fundus images in total are employed. In order to identify the hemorrhages, the suggested system is evaluated and achieved with an accuracy of 93.26%. For the given dataset, the outcomes are also contrasted with a few cutting-edge methods currently in use to ensure efficacy and superiority. Every experiment is carried out ten times and the results are taken into consideration. A comparative evaluation of various methods for detecting dot hemorrhages in DR is presented. The recommended method discovers hemorrhages more precisely and yields better results in less calculation time.

Dataset Analysis:

The Table 4.10 describes about the dataset used for testing and validation. A total of 3662 training images are shared as 80:20 for testing and validation respectively using cross entropy loss and LRelu activation function.

Table 4.10 Modeled parameters

Parameters	Values
Train Image Dataset	**3662**
Test Image Dataset	733
Validated Image Dataset	292
Final testing Dataset	**1928**
Loss Function	Cross Entropy Loss
Activation Function	LReLU, Sigmoid

A quantitative comparison between our suggested system and other approaches is shown in Table 4.11, which shows that even with a huge dataset, our technique performs better than the other algorithms.

Qureshi et al. [83] attained the greatest accuracy of 98% among the compared methods, whereas Zhang et al. [32] achieved 90.6%, Garcia et al. [33] reached 83.03%. But using APTOS datasets, our proposed method gives with an accuracy of 93.26%. Our better performance is attributed to our efficient modeling of hemorrhages, which improves identification over current approaches that mainly target dark spot areas like dot hemorrhages in retinal fundus images.

Table 4.11 Comparative analysis of the proposed model

Authors	Datasets	Method	Accuracy
Zhang et al. [32]	DIARETDB1	Multi-scale correlation filtering	90.6%
García et al. [63]	MESSIDOR	Four neural network	83.08%
Qureshi et al. [83]	EyePACS	ADL-CNN	98%
Mumtaz et al. [84]	DIARETDB1	Scale based	89%
Our Proposed Method	**APTOS**	**CNN**	**93.26%**

CHAPTER 5

MACHINE LEARNING METHODS FOR THE CLASSIFICATION OF VARIOUS STAGES OF DIABETIC RETINOPATHY

5.1 INTRODUCTION

Various machine learning algorithms like Random Forest, Logistic Regression and Support Vector Machines have been used to identify and classify the different phases of eye illness.

The objective of this study is to categorize the hemorrhages into two distinct forms of diabetic retinopathy: Non-proliferative (Early-stage) and Proliferative (Neovascular).

Various algorithms available for classifying the dot hemorrhage data acquired during segmentation, like:

- K-Nearest Neural Network (KNN)
- Naive bayes
- Logistic regression
- SVM
- Kernel SVM
- Random Forest
- Decision tree

5.2 MOTIVATION

In order to classify the nature of the DOT Hemorrhage such as normal, mild, moderate, severe has motivated to opt for utilizing different machine learning algorithms in combination with the activation function.

5.3 PROPOSED METHOD

Different stages of eye disease were classified using ML methods like logistic regression, support vector machines and random forest. Classification of DR comprises five stages: 1.normal, 2.mild, 3. moderate, 4.severe (NPDR) and 5. Advanced severe stage (PDR)

Classification

There are three steps involved in this process:

1) Training: Determining representative training location and using training sets to give quantitative analysis of every class type's features,

2) Classification method: The class that best describes a given set of data is used to group the data.

3) Output: The procedure is made up of an interpretive category matrix.

Random Forest is an ensemble learning method for regression & classification that employs multiple decision trees to boost model's accuracy and robustness. This method generates several decision trees and averages their forecasts to reduce overfitting and improve the generalization capacity of the model.

Random Forests (RF) is a tree-based classifier for classification. Tree-type classifiers are utilized in RF ensemble methods. They contain numerous forms of tree predictors, depends on the values for every tree in the forest of an independent and uniformly sampled random vector. They consist of different kinds of tree predictors, where the values of each tree in the forest are determined by a randomly selected, uniformly and independently-sampled vector.

It makes use of bagging to create a collection of classification trees. RF differs as of prior bagging algorithms in that it uses an arbitrary selection using predictor variables as candidate variables in the underlying classification trees to specify the split at each splitting node. Use a bootstrapped sample that was obtained from initial training set of data, it creates many classification and regression trees during training. After that, in order to calculate a split for every node, it only takes into account a randomly chosen subset of the input variables.

RF finds splits in predictor variables using the node impurity's Gini value. Every tree votes once for most well-liked class at input x during classification process. The trees with the highest classification accuracy cast the majority of votes to decide the classifier's output. It performs better than a number of tree-based algorithms due to its absence of overfitting and reduced sensitivity to noise. Computational complexity is decreased in RF since there is no tree pruning.

RF uses a huge number of trees in its ensemble, which allows it to manage input with high dimensions. Reducing correlation between the trees in ensemble is another goal of choosing random variables for splits, which produces inaccuracy rates that are comparable to Adaboost's but need far less computational work in real-world scenarios.

A pseudocode that describes how to construct a Random Forest classifier to identify diabetic retinopathy from eye images. This pseudocode assumes that you have a dataset of labeled images.

In a random forest, the decision trees are arranged in parallel. The number of trees determines how the train dataset is divided into bootstrap samples. Each tree receives a unique bootstrap sample, although some samples may occasionally overlap. Since we are bootstrapping with replacement, we sample a set of data and then replace it before sampling again as shown in figure 5.1. In the forest, every choice tree will expand to its maximum potential. We accept the compromise at the end in order to lessen overfitting, a problem that every decision tree will encounter.

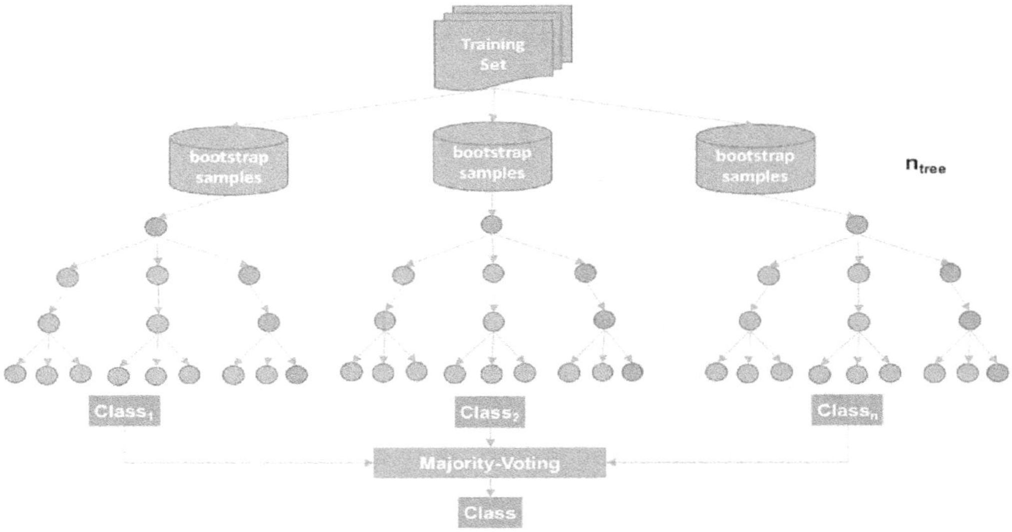

Figure 5.1 Random forest tree flow diagram

5.3.1 Random Forest

Pseudocode for Random Forest for Diabetic Retinopathy Detection

Step 1: Define functions for data loading and preprocessing

if file is an image:

load image

append image to image_list

return image_list

Step 2 : Function to preprocess images

for each image in image_list:

resize image to fixed size (e.g., 224x224)

normalize image (e.g., divide by 255)

extract features from image (e.g., using a pretrained CNN)

append processed image to preprocessed_images

return preprocessed_images

Step 3: Function for loading and preprocessing the data

for each subdirectory in dataset_path:

label = name of subdirectory (e.g., "no_dr", "mild_dr", etc.)

image_list = load_images_from_directory(subdirectory)

processed_images = preprocess_images(image_list)

append processed_images to images

*append [label]*len(processed_images) to labels*

return images, labels

Step 4: Split the dataset into sets for testing and training

Images for training and testing, label the trained and test data = split the train and test

(labels, images, size_train = ratio_train)

return the train images, test images, test labels, train labels

Step 5: Develop the Random Forest model

initialize randomforestclassifier with n_estimators=100, max_depth=10

fit the model to the train images and labels

return model

Step 6: Review the model

use the model to predict the test labels

accuracy = acc score (predictions, test labels)

return the accuracy

Step 7: Main function that execute the process

labels images = load and preprocess the data

training images, training labels, testing images, testing labels = split_dataset(images,

labels, train ratio=0.8)

model = train_random_forest(train_images, train_labels)

accuracy to evaluate the model (model, images and labels of test)

print the model accuracy

run the main function

call main()

5.3.2 Logistic Regression

ML techniques may be largely categorized into two classes: supervised and unsupervised. Principal Component Analysis and clustering algorithms are the most used unsupervised learning approaches. Unlike supervised algorithms, unsupervised methods do not require labeled data; instead, they identify patterns in the input data to predict or classify outputs.

A supervised algorithm for classification, logistic regression is employed to compute the likelihood that an event falls into a specific class. If the threshold probability is greater than 50%, the model predicts that the event is in the positive class; otherwise, it predicts that the event is in the negative class. The sigmoid logistic function, represented by the symbol σ, has an output bound that ranges from 0 to 1.

The model has to make a few general assumptions before using logistic regression:

- It is error-free when measuring independent variables.
- Data are independent of each other.
- There is a binomial distribution for errors.
- There are no significant variables left out or superfluous variables added in.
- Independent variables do not combine in a linear fashion.
- The independent variables' logistic function determines the true conditional probability.

Logistic regression, along with linear regression, is unable to model nominal type data, despite the fact that several data sets contain it. This can be avoided by computing a dummy variable. One way to prevent perfect multicollinearity is to eliminate one of a data type's dummy variables. In addition, multicollinearity might influence the interpretation of the logistic regression model's independent coefficients and the estimation of the dependent variables if the correlation coefficient of many independent variables is high (>0.8).

 # Pseudocode for Logistic Regression for Diabetic Retinopathy Classification

Step 1: Import necessary libraries

Step 2: Define functions for data loading and preprocessing

Step 3: Function to load images from a directory

for each file in directory_path:

if file is an image:

image = load image from file

append image to image_list

return image_list

Step 4: Function to preprocess images

for each image in image_list:

resized_image = resize image to fixed size (224x224)

normalized_image = normalize resized_image (divide by 255)

features = extract features from normalized_image (e.g., using a pretrained cnn)

append features to preprocessed_images

return preprocessed_images

Step 5: Function to load and preprocess data

for each subdirectory in dataset_path:

label = name of subdirectory (e.g., "no_dr", "mild_dr")

image_list = load_images_from_directory(subdirectory)

processed_images = preprocess_images(image_list)

append processed_images to images

*append [label] * length(processed_images) to labels*

return images, labels

Step 6: Split the dataset into training and testing sets

train_images, test_images, train_labels, test_labels = train_test_split(images, labels, train_size=train_ratio)

return train_images, train_labels, test_images, test_labels

Step 7: Train the Logistic Regression model

model = initialize logisticregression(max_iter=1000)

fit model on train_images, train_labels

return model

Step 8: Evaluate the model

predictions = predict test_labels using model

accuracy = accuracy_score(test_labels, predictions)

return accuracy

Step 9: Main function to execute the steps

train_images, train_labels, test_images, test_labels = split_dataset(images, labels,

train_ratio=0.8)

model = train_logistic_regression(train_images, train_labels)

accuracy = evaluate_model(model, test_images, test_labels)

print "model accuracy:", accuracy

Step 10: Execute the main function

CALL main()

5.3.3 Support Vector Machine

SVM is a highly advanced ML technique commonly employed for classification purposes, including diabetic retinopathy classification, a diabetes-related eye complication. Below is an outline of how the SVM method can be applied to classify diabetic retinopathy:

Data collection: First step in the preparation process to acquire a labeled dataset of retinal images categorized by the severity of DR. These images can be classed into various categories as mentioned earlier.

Preprocessing: It is imperative to perform preprocessing on the images to make sure the SVM model can use them. This entails reframing, returning to normal and maybe boosting disease-specific features like hemorrhages, blood vessels or exudates.

Feature extraction: Since SVM performs best on numerical data, it's important to detect and extract useful properties from the images. This could entail approaches like color histograms, texture analysis, or convolutional neural networks for DL based feature extraction.

Selecting the Kernel: SVM can handle non-linear correlations in the data by utilizing a range of kernel functions, like linear, polynomial and radial basis function (RBF). Because of its capacity to handle intricate, high-dimensional feature spaces, an RBF kernel is frequently utilized for the classification of DR.

Model Training: The SVM model is trained using a labeled dataset. During training, the algorithm identifies optimal hyperplane to effectively separate the various kinds of DR. The objective is to optimize the margin between classes, ensuring the model performs well.

Handling Class Imbalance: Databases on diabetic retinopathy are frequently unbalanced, showing a higher proportion of severe cases than of moderate or nonexistent cases. To rectify this imbalance, methods such as applying a weighted SVM or oversampling or under sampling might be used.

Cross-validation: During the training phase, k-fold cross validation techniques are employed to ensure the model's performance on unfamiliar data.

Metrics of Performance: The metrics employed to assess the performance of SVM model encompass accuracy, precision, F1-score, recall and area under the ROC curve. These metrics assess the model's capacity to differentiate between various stages of diabetic retinopathy.

Benefits of Classifying DR Using SVM:

- SVM is a suitable choice for situations involving a large no. of features, which is frequently the case in medical image analysis. It also works well in three-dimensional space.
- Prevent against overfitting: SVM's objective of maximizing the margin between classes helps in preventing overfitting.
- Flexibility with Kernels: Depending on the kernel selected, SVM may effectively represent complex decision boundaries, which is useful for the complex patterns seen in retinal images.

Pseudocode for Support Vector Machine for Diabetic Retinopathy Classification

Step 1: Import necessary libraries

Step 2: Load the dataset

- Initialize an empty list data

- Read labels_file into a DataFrame labels

- For each img_name in labels ['image']:

- Construct img_path using os.path.join(image_dir, img_name)

- Open image at img_path using Image.open

- Append the image as a numpy array to data

- Return data as a numpy array and labels ['label'].values

Step 3: Preprocess the images

- Initialize an empty list processed_images

- For each img in images:

- Resize img to 223x224

- Convert img to a numpy array and normalize by dividing by 255.0

- Flatten the image and append to processed_images

- Return processed_images as a numpy array

Step 4: Load and preprocess the dataset

- Split the preprocessed images and labels into training and testing sets using train_test_split

Step 5. Initialize the SVM classifier

- Create an instance of SVC with kernel set to 'linear'

Step 6: Train the SVM classifier

- Fit the SVM classifier on the training data

Step 7: Evaluate the classifier

- Predict the labels for the test set using the trained SVM classifier

- Calculate accuracy and precision using the true and predicted labels

- Print the calculated evaluation metrics

Step 8: Tune the hyperparameters

- Define a parameter grid with different values for C, gamma, and kernel

- Use GridSearchCV with the parameter grid to find the best hyperparameters

- Fit the GridSearchCV on the training data and print the best parameters

Step 9: Save the trained model

- Use joblib to serialize and save the trained SVM model to disk

Step 10: Load and predict new images

- Load the SVM model from model_path using joblib

- Open new_image_path using Image.open

- Preprocess the new image using preprocess_images

- Predict the label for the preprocessed new image using the loaded SVM model

- Return the predicted label

5.4 FINDINGS AND ANALYSIS OF EXPERIMENTAL ASSESSMENT

Derived from the data sources of APTOS 2019 Blindness Detection database, the Table 5.1 presents the classifiers performance with the label ID's results in recognizing dot hemorrhages. The images have been categorized into the relevant folders based on stages and level of diabetic retinal dot hemorrhages by given dataset file as shown in Figure 5.2. The matching images are located in five directories.

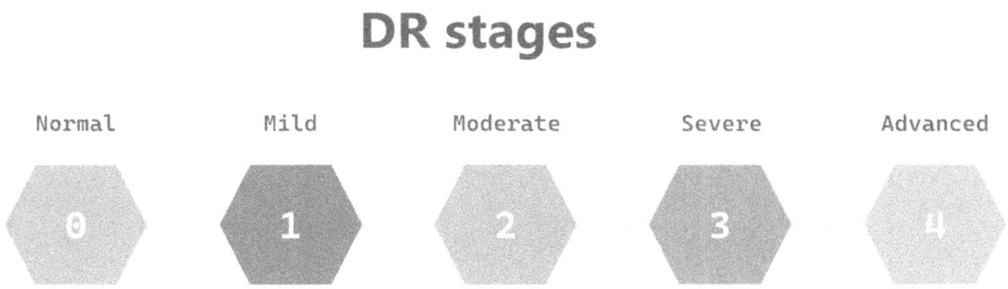

Figure 5.2 Stages wise folder label

Table 5.1 Classifiers performance

S No.	Label Id	Diagnosis	Binary-type	Stage
0	000cl434d8d7	2	DH	Moderate
1	001639a390f0	4	DH	Proliferate-DR
2	0024cdab0cle	1	DH	Mild
3	6bc23af521fs	0	No-DH	No-DR
4	06be1092a062	0	No-DH	No-DR

The training dataset of 3662 images is categorized into various stages, including normal, mild, moderate, severe and advanced stage proliferative DR, as depicted in Figure 5.3.

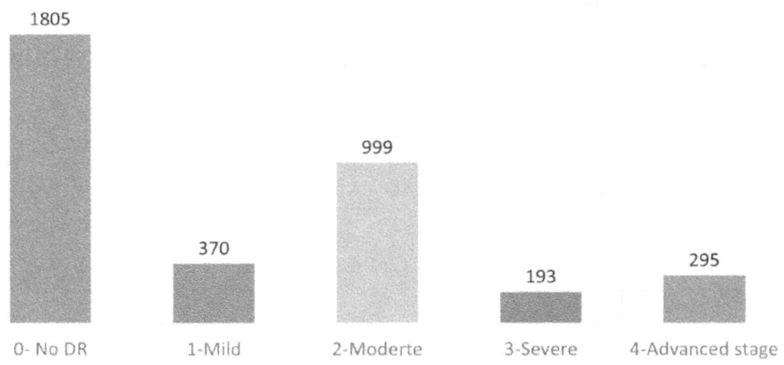

Figure 5.3 APTOS dataset category wise count

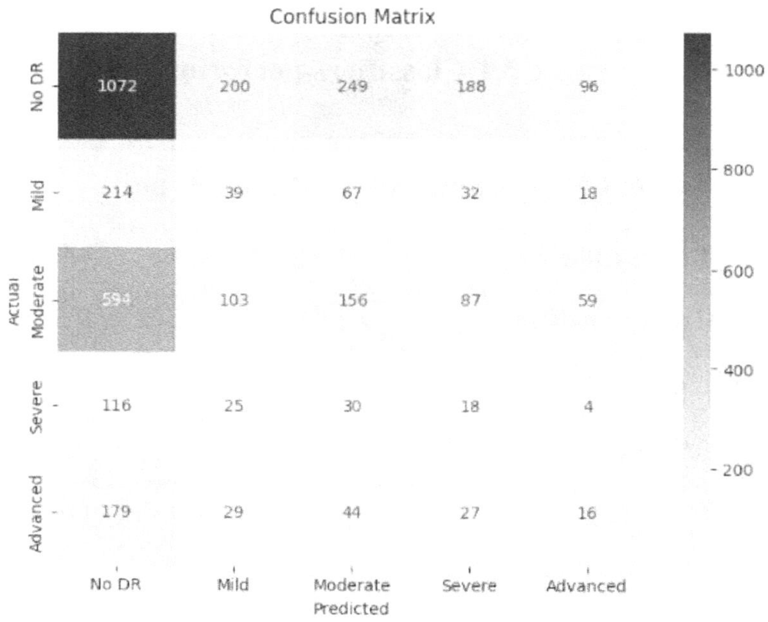

Figure 5.4 Confusion matrix APTOS dataset

The confusion matrix is a vital instrument for assessing classification models since it offers a more thorough perspective of model performance compared to accuracy alone. Figure 5.4 displays the Confusion Matrix for APTOS datasets, providing a detailed analysis of the different stages of diabetic retinopathy.

5.4.1 APTOS database

Source of Data:

The data from Kaggle's APTOS 2019 Blindness Detection dataset comprises 5 files, totaling 9.52 GB in size.

i. The test_images directory contains 1,928 test images.

ii. The train images directory contains 3662 images.

iii. Sample_submission.csv (28.26 KB).

iv. The path to the test images as id_code in test.csv (24.48 KB).

v. Path to training images as id_code and target class labels as diagnosis are contained in the train.csv file (53.66 KB).

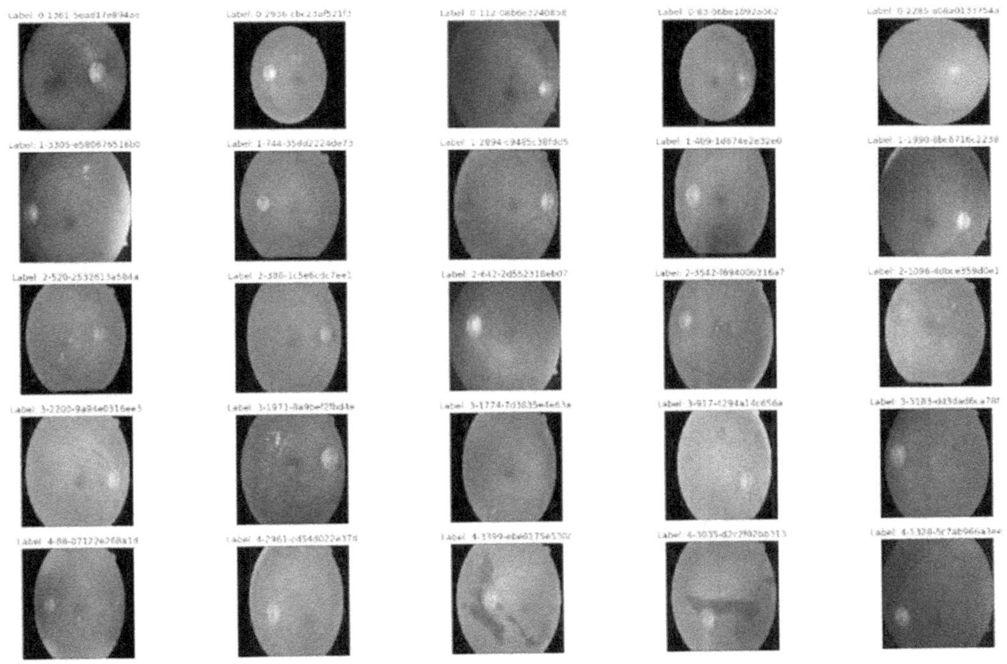

Figure 5.5 (a) APTOS dataset sample images with label ID's

Figure 5.5(a) illustrates the performance of different classifiers on APTOS dataset consists of 3662 photos for training and 1928 images for testing. The label ID's represent different diagnostic stages, such as normal (No-DR), mild, moderate, severe and proliferative DR, categorized as DH or NO-DH and Figure 5.5(b) shows with stage-wise sample images.

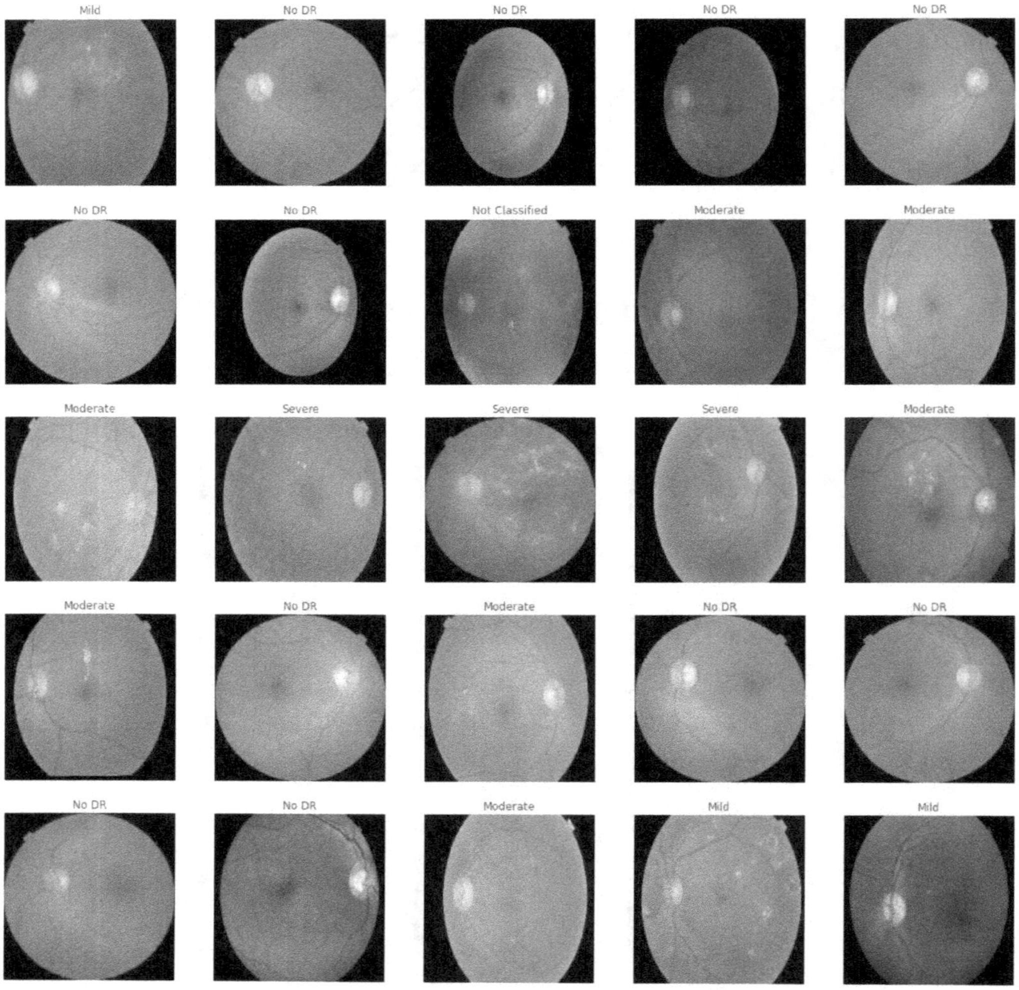

Figure 5.5 (b) APTOS dataset with stage wise label

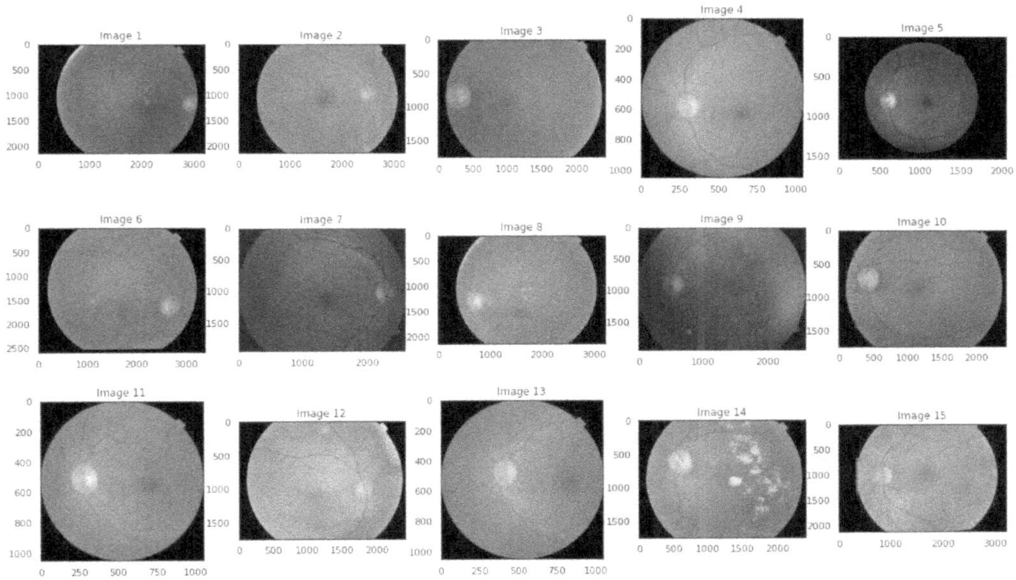

Figure 5.6 A sample of 15 images with different dimension

Both the training and test images lack a standardized format. To avoid losing crucial pixel information, we need to ensure that all images are adjusted to a consistent resolution, preferably a high one. The Figure 5.6 shows the sampled images of APTOS database based on the following conditions.

- Images characterized by a mostly dark color palette Illumination: The presence of very dark images may lead our algorithm to make inaccurate classifications.

- Images displaying varying degrees of color inversion: Some of the photographs exhibit distinct variations in color tones, such as blue, pink and green.

- The collection contains images with four distinct types of uneven cropping.

- ➢ Square crop: Square image with No cropping needed
- ➢ Vertical crop: Rectangular image with lossy vertical cropping
- ➢ Tight crop: Images with tight cropping (lossy vertical and horizontal cropping)
- ➢ Space crop: Images with more informative pixels.

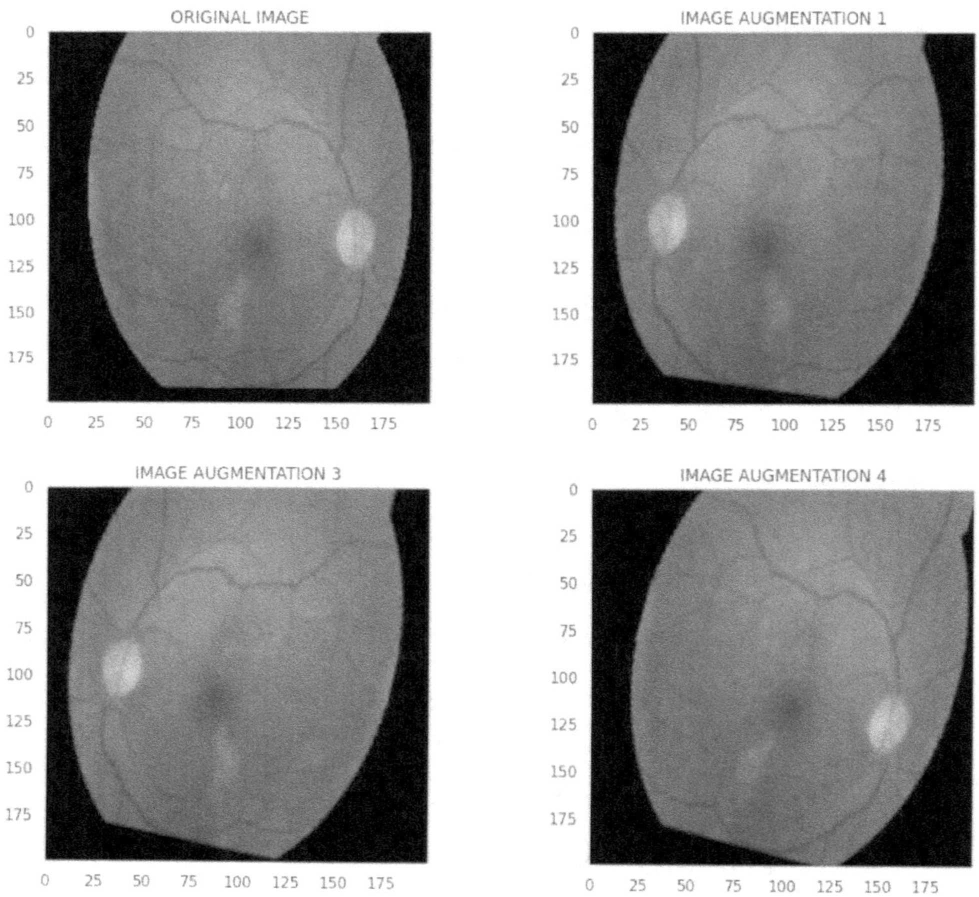

Figure 5.7 Image augmentation of APTOS dataset

Image Augmentation:

Geometric transformations method are employed to increase the size of the dataset by undergoing random flipping of an image, cropping, scaling or rotation shown in Figure 5.7.

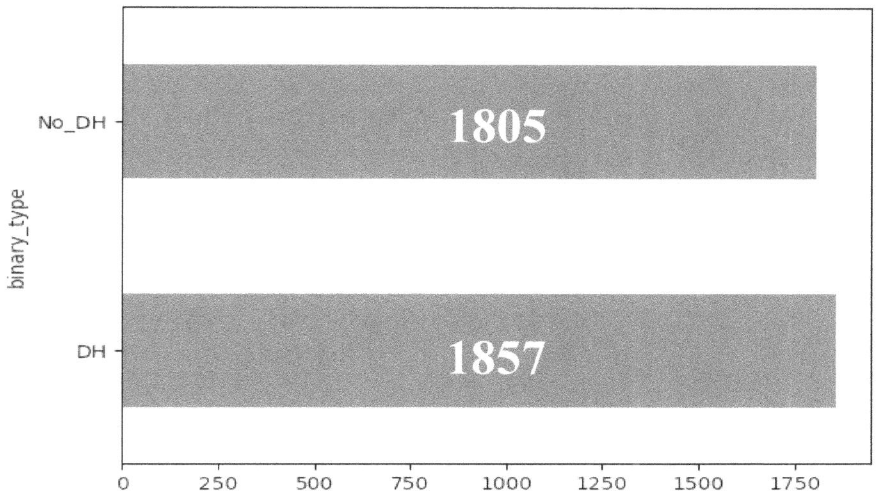

Figure 5.8 DH/No DH – binary type

Figure 5.8 presents the binary classification of DR, distinguishing between 1857 images labeled as DH and 1805 images labeled as No-DH.

Criteria for evaluating performance:

The outcomes of our suggested approach are evaluated using several measures like accuracy (Acc), losses and Receiver Operating Characteristic curve, sometimes referred to as Area under Curve (AUC). These characteristics are utilized to evaluate the performance of proposed system in relation to other algorithms. The metrics are defined in the following Equations 5.1.

$$Acc = \frac{(TP + TN)}{(TP + FP + TN + FN)} \times 100\% \tag{5.1}$$

Table 5.2 DR_DH stage wise classification percentage

CLASSES	NO. OF TRAINING DATA	NO. OF TEST DATA	NO OF CORRECT CLASSIFICATIONS	% OF CORRECT CLASSIFICATIONS
0 - No_DR	1805	1390	1283	92.3%
1 - Mild	370	132	121	91.6%
2 - Moderate	999	206	191	92.7%
3 - Severe	193	82	75	91.4%
4 - Proliferate_DR	295	118	112	93.2%
	3662	**1928**	**1782**	**92.4%**

The Table 5.2 represents the classes over the available dataset to classify the percentage of correct classification. The training and testing datasets are compared stage by stage, as shown in Figure 5.9.

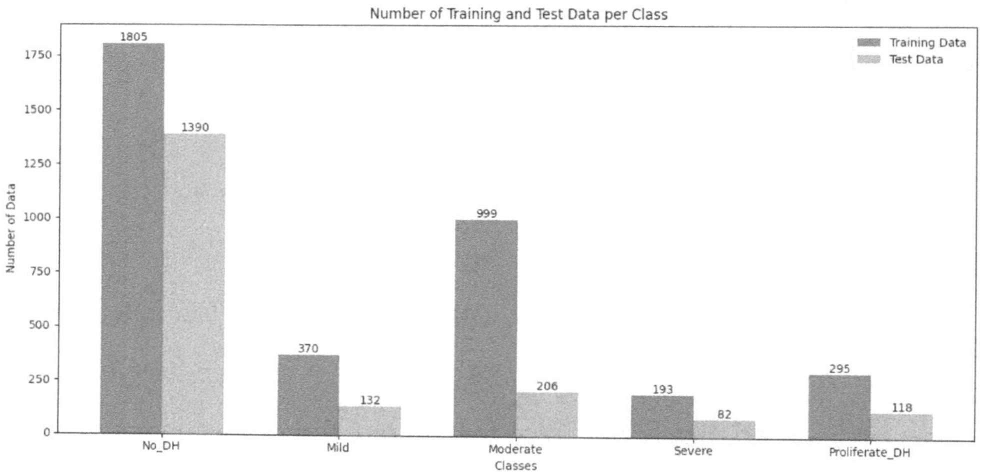

Figure 5.9 Number of training and testing data per class/stage

The validation of test images, comparing the actual input images with the predicted output images, is shown in Figure 5.10, presented as a percentage across various stages.

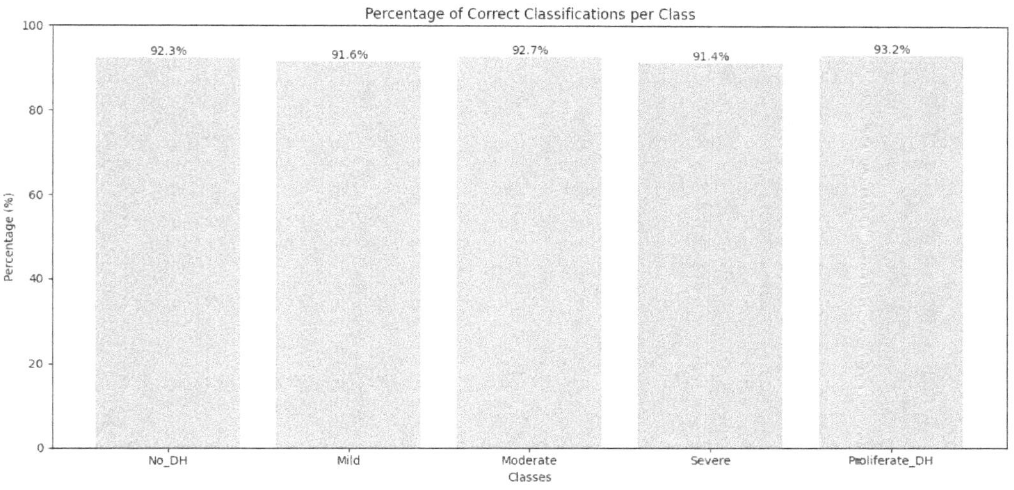

Figure 5.10 Percentage of correct classifications

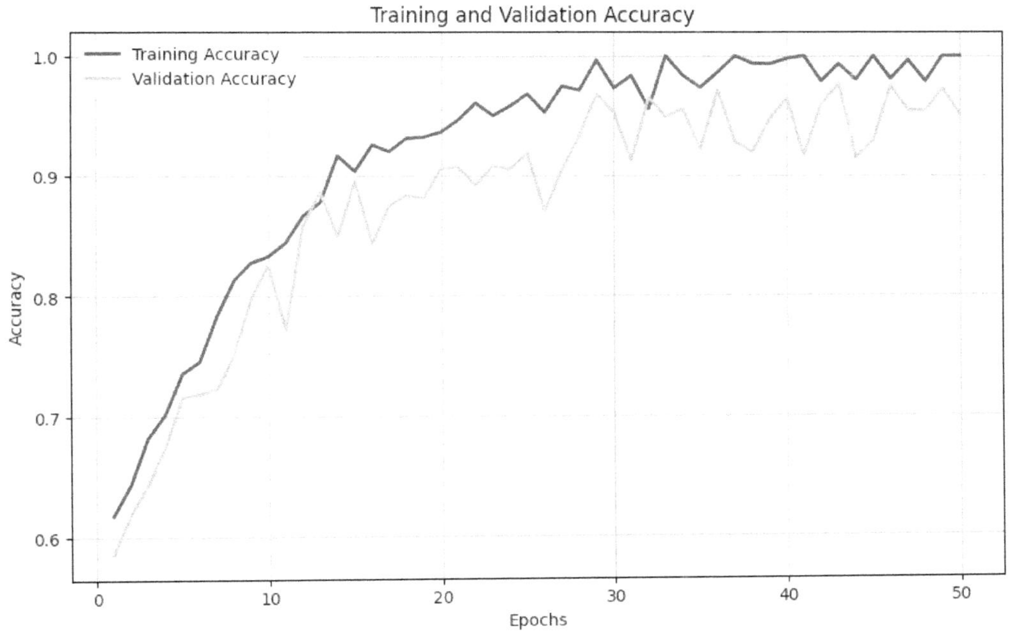

Figure 5.11 Training and validation accuracy

The Figure 5.11 depicts about the training versus validation accuracy. As the accuracy increases with the number of epoch increases.

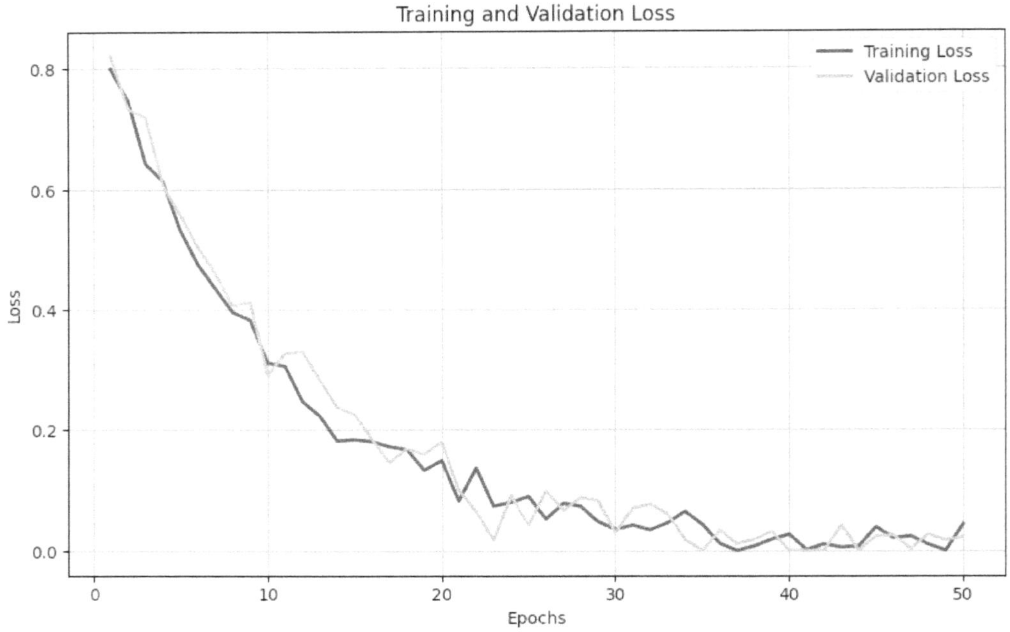

Figure 5.12 Training and validation loss

The Figure 5.12 depicts about the training versus validation loss. As the number of epoch increases the loss decreases.

The Receiver Operating Characteristic curve visually represents a model's performance across different thresholds. It is generated by calculating the True Positive Rate (TPR) and False Positive Rate (FPR) for each possible threshold or at specific intervals and plotting TPR against FPR for all as shown in Figure 5.13. A perfect model, achieving a TPR of 1.0 and an FPR of 0.0, would appear as a single point at coordinates (0, 1) on the graph, without considering any other factors.

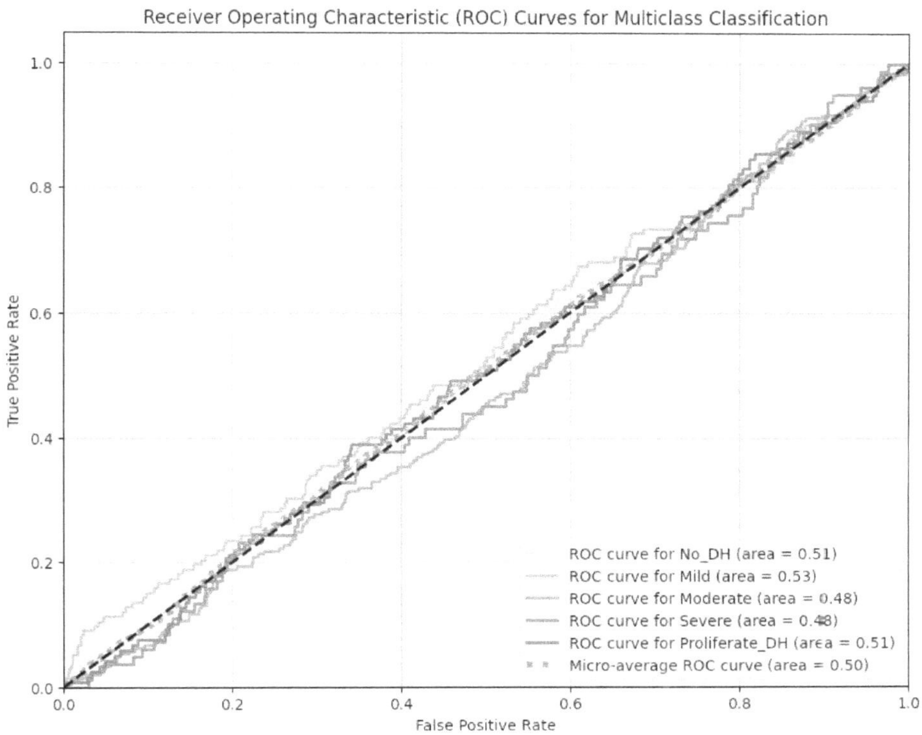

Figure 5.13 ROC curve for multiclass classification

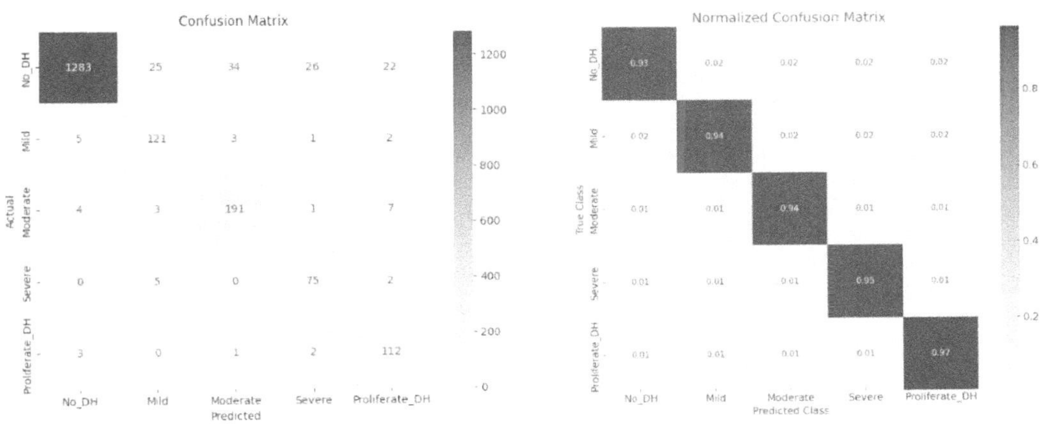

Figure 5.14 Confusion matrix

a) DR_DH stages b) Normalized output

Our proposed system's performance is further shown using the Confusion Matrix for the APTOS datasets, which highlights the accurate prediction of various stages of DR, as illustrated in Figure 5.14.

Table 5.3 Classification model of DR_DH

Model	Binary _type	Normal	Mild	Moderate	Severe	PDR
Logistic Regression	DH	88.1%	89.3%	93.6%	86.4%	76.7%
Support Vector machine	DH	90.5%	90.5%	83.6%	87.4%	84.1%
Random Forest	DH	92.3%	91.6%	92.7%	91.4%	93.2%

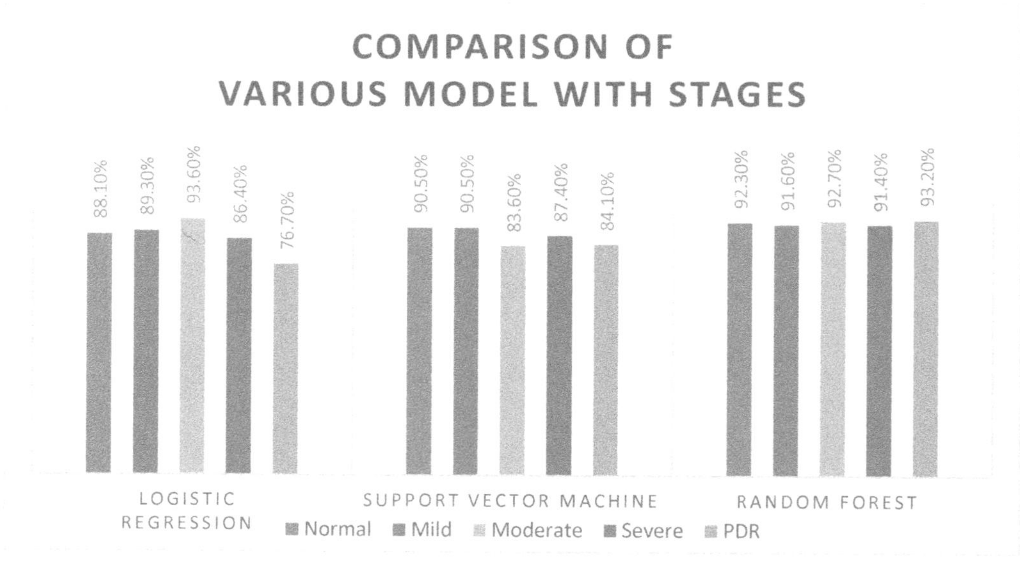

Figure 5.15 Comparison of various model with stages

In Table 5.3 and Figure 5.15 displays the classification of Diabetic Retinopathy Dot Hemorrhage (DH) across different categories using ML algorithms, including Random Forest, Linear Regression and Support Vector Machine. Among these, the Random Forest model demonstrates the highest accuracy compared to others. The proposed model achieved a 93.2% accuracy with the corresponding loss of 18.4%.

Prediction:

307.1s	20	Accuracy: 0.9327272772789001
305.1s	21	Vision loss: 0.18484
309.2s	22	Dot hemorrhage is detected.

5.5 SUMMARY

Using convolutional neural network technology is advised for promptly identifying diabetic dot hemorrhage in retinal fundus through dynamic image comparison. While the suggested work is **successful in classifying dot hemorrhage**, further improvements in the form of additional classifiers will be required to raise the accuracy rate even further.

In order to maximize the recognition rate with the least amount of time complexity, the system's performance is evaluated using a vast amount of records and intelligence techniques. The comparative analysis of dynamic imaging dot hemorrhage detects and classifies with an average accuracy of **92.4%** for the proposed method.

CHAPTER 6

CONCLUSION AND FUTURE WORK

Diabetic retinopathy is a condition that occurs as a result of prolonged diabetes, is among the most persistent complications associated with the disease. It is currently a prominent worldwide cause of vision loss. On a global scale, the prevalence of diabetes cases is rising and among all patients, diagnosing DR is getting harder and harder. The retina suffers vascular and neuronal damage as a result of vitreous hemorrhage. The only ways for diabetes individuals to prevent the dangerous repercussions of the disease are routine check-ups for an early diagnosis and strict blood sugar management. The main cause is because in its early stages, the illness seldom ever exhibits any symptoms. Regular ocular examinations are the sole method to identify DR at these stages.

Getting routine eye exams is the only approach to identify DR at this stage. For all diabetic patients, the current manual DR diagnostic techniques are currently insufficient in terms of diagnosis. To achieve our primary objective of creating an automated technique for detecting DR, we have attempted to address a number of significant problems related to the use of retinal fundus images for the classification of DR.

Chapter 3 discussed various algorithms related to the Diabetic Retinopathy (DR) using Dot Hemorrhages to find the accuracy.

Image classification, pattern recognition, ML and DL are the main methods used. Using DL techniques like CNN VGG16 model is the finest method for classifying the DR. The following problems that are addressed the classification problem utilizing fundus pictures for DR:

i. Local minima and CNN's vanishing gradient issue are brought about by back-propagation.

ii. Precisely and completely removing characteristics from the fundus images

iii. To develop an automated system capable of recognizing DR is the primary objective.

Chapter 4, a variety of neural network architectures have been suggested for the identification of dot hemorrhages in order to achieve improved accuracy.

APTOS datasets are used to process a total of 3662 retinal fundus pictures. The proposed method is assessed and reaches an accuracy of 93.26% in identifying the hemorrhages using the VGG16 model. In this specific experiment, LReLu turned out to be the best activation function for CNN picture classification. The study discovered that in CNN situations, the Adam and Adadelta optimizers produce above 50% excellent accuracy values.

To assure efficacy and superiority, the results are also compared to the methods that are currently applied to the given dataset. Ten trials are conducted for each experiment and the outcomes are taken into account. The effectiveness of existing methods for diabetic retinopathy dot hemorrhage identification is compared with our suggested approach. It takes less time to calculate and produces better results when using the proposed technique to identify hemorrhages.

Chapter 5 proposes the classification of the presence of dot hemorrhage using Machine learning algorithms to attain enhanced accuracy.

Several ML methods, including Random Forest, Support Vector Machines and Logistic Regression, have been employed to identify and classify the several stages of ocular disease. Proliferative diabetic retinopathy (PDR), mild, moderate and severe non-proliferative diabetic retinopathy (NPDR) and both are the five categories into which this work attempts to categorize hemorrhage. The proposed work successfully classifies dot hemorrhage; nevertheless, to increase the accuracy rate even further, more modifications in the form of additional classifiers would be needed. To optimize recognition rate while minimizing time complexity, the system's performance is evaluated using a wealth of data and intelligence methodologies. For the suggested technique, the comparative analysis of dynamic imaging dot hemorrhage identifies and classifies with an accuracy of 92.4%.

FUTURE SCOPE:

Individuals with diabetes, regardless of the kind of diabetes, need to have frequent retinal screenings to diagnose and treat DR in a timely manner. Retinopathy screening is often performed in a physician's office by qualified medical personnel. Recent times have seen the rise of smartphones, the DR test can be carried out based on retinal imaging which can be potentially more accessible, economical and effective method of diagnosing DR. In diabetic retinopathy various lesions like Hard and soft Exudates can also be screened by single diagnosis.

REFERENCES

[1] Katsarou A., Gudbjörnsdottir S., Rawshani A., Dabelea D., Bonifacio E., Anderson B.J., Jacobsen L.M., Schatz, D.A., Lernmark Å. (2017), "Type 1 diabetes mellitus", Nature reviews Disease primers, Vol.3(1), pp.1-17.

[2] Sikder N., Masud M., Bairagi A.K., Arif A.S.M., Nahid A.A., Alhumyani H.A. (2021), "Severity Classification of Diabetic Retinopathy Using an Ensemble Learning Algorithm through Analyzing Retinal Images", Symmetry, Vol. 13(4), p.670.

[3] ChawlaAastha et al. (2016), "Microvascular and macrovascular complications in diabetes mellitus: Distinct or continuum", Indian journal of endocrinology and metabolism, Vol. 20(4), pp. 546-51.

[4] Zimmerman R. (2016), "Diabetes mellitus: management of microvascular and macrovascular complications" Cleveland Clinic: Centers for Continuing Education.

[5] Sun Y., Smith L.E. (2018), "Retinal vasculature in development and diseases", Annual review of vision science, Vol. 4, pp.101-122.

[6] Das A., Stroud S., Mehta A., Rangasamy S. (2015), "New treatments for diabetic retinopathy", Diabetes, Obesity and Metabolism, Vol. 17(3), pp.219-230.

[7] Rajkumar R.S., Selvarani A.G., Ranjithkumar S. (2020), "Comprehensive Study on Diabetic Retinopathy", Soft Computing for Problem Solving, pp. 155-163.

[8] Wong T.Y. and Sabanayagam C. (2020), Strategies to tackle the global burden of diabetic retinopathy: from epidemiology to artificial intelligence. Ophthalmologica, 243(1), pp.9-20.

[9] Karst S.G., Lammer J., Radwan S.H., Kwak H., Silva P.S., Burns S.A., Aiello L.P., Sun J.K. (2018), "Characterization of in vivo retinal lesions of diabetic retinopathy using adaptive optics scanning laser ophthalmoscopy", International journal of endocrinology.

[10] Long S., Chen J., Hu A. et al. (2020), "Microaneurysms detection in color fundus images using machine learning based on directional local contrast", Bio Med Eng OnLine, Vol.19, pp.21.

[11] Wang, H, Hsu, W, Goh, KG & Lee, M (2000), 'An effective approach to detect lesions in color retinal images', IEEE Conference on Computer Vision and Pattern Recognition, vol. 2, pp. 181–186.

[12] Amin J., Sharif M., Yasmin M. (2016), "A review on recent developments for detection of diabetic retinopathy", Scientifica.

[13] Shi Z., He L., Suzuki K., Nakamura T., Itoh H. (2009), "Survey on neural networks used for medical image processing", International journal of computational science, Vol. 3(1), pp.86.

[14] Kamilaris A., Prenafeta-Boldú F.X. (2018), "A review of the use of convolutional neural networks in agriculture", The Journal of Agricultural Science, Vol. 156(3), pp.312-322.

[15] Rawat W., Wang, Z. (2017), "Deep convolutional neural networks for image classification: A comprehensive review", Neural computation, Vol. 29(9), pp.2352-2449.

[16] Agatonovic-Kustrin S., Beresford R. (2000), "Basic concepts of artificial neural network (ANN) modeling and its application in pharmaceutical research", Journal of pharmaceutical and biomedical analysis, Vol. 22(5), pp.717-727.

[17] Puri M., Solanki A., Padawer T., Tipparaju S.M., Moreno W.A., Pathak Y. (2016), "Introduction to artificial neural network (ANN) as a predictive tool for drug design, discovery, delivery, and disposition: Basic concepts and modelling", Artificial neural network for drug design, delivery and disposition,pp. 3-13.

[18] Sengupta S., Basak S., Saikia P., Paul S., Tsalavoutis V., Atiah F., Ravi V., Peters A. (2020), "A review of deep learning with special emphasis on architectures, applications and recent trends", Knowledge-Based Systems, Vol. 194, pp.105596.

[19] Sonam Solkar, Lekha Das (2017), "A New Approach for Detection and Classification of Diabetic Retinopathy Using PNN and SVM Classifiers" IOSR Journal of Computer Engineering (IOSR-JCE), Volume 19, Issue 5, PP 62-68.

[20] Akhtar N., Ragavendran U. (2020), "Interpretation of intelligence in CNN-pooling processes: a methodological survey", Neural computing and applications, Vol. 32(3), pp.879-898.

[21] Lee C.Y., Gallagher P.W., Tu, Z. (2016), "Generalizing pooling functions in convolutional neural networks: Mixed, gated, and tree", Artificial intelligence and statistics, pp. 464-472.

[22] Song Z., Yan L., Rong S., Zhenguang C., Jianyong Y., Chao Z., Qing J. (2018), "A sparsity-based stochastic pooling mechanism for deep convolutional neural networks", Neural Networks, Vol.105, pp.340-345.

[23] Zhao H., Fuxian L., Han Z., Zhibing L. (2019), "Research on a learning rate with energy index in deep learning", Neural Networks, Vol.110, pp.225-231.

[24] Sharma A. (2018), "Guided stochastic gradient descent algorithm for inconsistent datasets", Applied Soft Computing, Vol.73, pp.1068-1080.

[25] Kingma D. P., Jimmy B. (2014), "Adam: A method for stochastic optimization",arXiv preprint arXiv: 1412.6980.

[26] Zeiler M. D. (2012), "ADADELTA: an adaptive learning rate method", arXiv preprint arXiv: 1212.5701.

[27] Casanova R., Saldana S., Chew E.Y., Danis R.P., Greven C.M., Ambrosius W.T. (2014), "Application of random forests methods to diabetic retinopathy classification analyses", PLOS one, Vol. 9(6), pp.e98587.

[28] Priya R., Aruna P (2013), "Diagnosis of diabetic retinopathy using machine learning techniques", ICTACT Journal on soft computing, Vol. 3(4), pp.563-575.

[29] Gharaibeh N., Al-Hazaimeh O.M., Al-Naami B., Nahar K.M. (2018), "An effective image processing method for detection of diabetic retinopathy diseases from retinal fundus images", International Journal of Signal and Imaging Systems Engineering, Vol.11(4), pp.206-216.

[30] Lam C., Yi D., Guo M., Lindsey T. (2018), "Automated detection of diabetic retinopathy using deep learning", AMIA Summits on Translational Science Proceedings, pp.147-155.

[31] Adem K. (2018), "Exudate detection for diabetic retinopathy with circular Hough transformation and convolutional neural networks", Expert Systems with Applications, Vol.114, pp.289-295.

[32] Zhang W., Zhong J., Yang S., Gao Z., Hu, J., Chen Y., Yi Z. (2019), "Automated identification and grading system of diabetic retinopathy using deep neural networks", Knowledge-Based Systems, Vol. 175, pp.12-25.

[33] Shanthi T., Sabeenian R.S. (2019), "Modified Alexnet architecture for classification of diabetic retinopathy images",Computers & Electrical Engineering,Vol. 76, pp.56-64.

[34] Kathiresan S., Sait A.R.W., Gupta D., Lakshmanaprabu S.K., Khanna A., Pandey H.M. (2020), "Automated detection and classification of fundus diabetic retinopathy images using synergic deep learning model", Pattern Recognition Letters.

[35] Gayathri S., Gopi V.P., Palanisamy P. (2020), "A lightweight CNN for Diabetic Retinopathy classification from fundus images",Biomedical Signal Processing and Control, Vol. 62, pp.102115.

[36] Chen W., Yang B., Li J., Wang J. (2020), "An approach to detecting diabetic retinopathy based on integrated shallow convolutional neural networks", IEEE Access, Vol. 8, pp.178552-178562.

[37] Pao S.I., Lin H.Z., Chien K.H., Tai M.C., Chen J.T., Lin G.M. (2020), "Detection of diabetic retinopathy using bichannel convolutional neural network",Journal of Ophthalmology.

[38] Hemanth D.J, Deperlioglu O, Kose, U. (2020), "An enhanced diabetic retinopathy detection and classification approach using deep convolutional neural network", Neural Computing and Applications, Vol. 32(3), pp.707-721.

[39] Chaturvedi S.S., Gupta K., Ninawe V., Prasad P.S. (2020), "Automated diabetic retinopathy grading using deep convolutional neural network", Pattern Recognition letters, Vol. 135, pp. 293-298.

[40] Roychowdhury S., Koozekanani D.D., Parhi K.K. (2013), "DREAM: Diabetic Retinopathy analysis using machine learning", IEEE journal of biomedical and health informatics, Vol. 18(5), pp.1717-1728.

[41] Lachure J., Deorankar A.V., Lachure S., Gupta S., Jadhav R. (2015), "Diabetic Retinopathy using morphological operations and machine learning", IEEE International Advance Computing Conference (IACC), pp. 617-622.

[42] Tsao H.Y., Chan P.Y., Su E.C.Y. (2018), "Predicting diabetic retinopathy and identifying interpretable biomedical features bioinformatics, Vol. 19(9), pp.283.

[43] Carrera E.V., González A., Carrera R. (2017), "Automated detection of diabetic retinopathy using SVM", IEEE XXIV International Conference on Electronics, Electrical Engineering and Computing (INTERCON), pp. 1-4.

[44] Mansour R.F., Abdelrahim, E.M., Al-Johani A.S. (2013), "Identification of Diabetic Retinal Exudates in Digital Color Images Using Support Vector Machine", Journal of Intelligent Learning Systems and Applications, Vol. 5, pp.135-142.

[45] Aravind C., Ponnibala M., Vijayachitra S. (2013), "Automatic detection of microaneurysms and classification of diabetic retinopathy images using SVM technique", International Journal of Computer Applications, Vol.975, pp.8887.

[46] Saha R., Chowdhury A.R., Banerjee S. (2016), "Diabetic retinopathy related lesions detection and classification using machine learning technology", International Conference on Artificial Intelligence and Soft Computing, pp. 734-745.

[49] Bhatkar A.P., Kharat G.U. (2015), "Detection of diabetic retinopathy in retinal images using MLP classifier", IEEE international symposium on nanoelectronic and information systems, pp. 331-335.

[50] Alazzam, Malik Bader, Fawaz Alassery and Ahmed H. Almulihi. (2021), "Identification of Diabetic Retinopathy through Machine Learning." Mob. Inf. Syst. 1155116:1-1155116:8.

[51] Gayathri, S., Krishna, A.K., Gopi, V.P. and Palanisamy, P. (2020), "Automated binary and multiclass classification of diabetic retinopathy using haralick and multiresolution features", IEEE Access, 8, pp.57497-57504.

[52] Mujeeb Rahman, K.K., Nasor, M. and Imran, A. (2022), "Automatic Screening of Diabetic Retinopathy Using Fundus Images and Machine Learning Algorithms. Diagnostics, 12(9), p.2262.

[53] Narayanan, B.N., Hardie, R.C., De Silva, M.S. and Kueterman, N.K. (2020), "Hybrid machine learning architecture for automated detection and grading of retinal images for diabetic retinopathy", Journal of Medical Imaging, 7(3), pp.034501-034501.

[54] Jadhav, Ambaji S. et al. (2020), "Optimal feature selection-based diabetic retinopathy detection using improved rider optimization algorithm enabled with deep learning." *Evolutionary Intelligence,* 14: 1431 - 1448.

[55] Ramasamy L.K., Padinjappurathu S.G., Kadry S., Damaševičius, R. (2021), "Detection of diabetic retinopathy using a fusion of textural and ridgelet features of retinal images and sequential minimal optimization classifier", PeerJ computer science, Vol. 7, pp.e456.

[56] Jayanthi J., Jayasankar T., Krishnaraj N., Prakash N.B., Sagai Francis Britto A., Vinoth Kumar K. (2021), "An intelligent particle swarm optimization with convolutional neural network for diabetic retinopathy classification model", Journal of Medical Imaging and Health Informatics, Vol. 11(3), pp.803-809.

[57] Mateen M., Wen J., Song S. and Huang Z. (2019), "Fundus image classification using VGG-19 architecture with PCA and SVD", Symmetry, Vol. 11(1), p.1.

[58] Li Y.H., Ye N.N., Chen, S.J., Chung, Y.C. (2019), "Computer-assisted diagnosis for diabetic retinopathy based on fundus images using deep convolutional neural network. Mobile Information Systems, pages: 1-14.

[59] Lin G.M., Chen M.J., Yeh C.H., Lin Y.Y., Kuo H.Y., Lin M.H., Chen M.C., Lin S.D., Gao Y., Ran A., Cheung C.Y. (2018), "Transforming retinal photographs to entropy images in deep learning to improve automated detection for diabetic retinopathy", Journal of ophthalmology.

[60] Wan S., Liang Y., Zhang, Y. (2018), "Deep convolutional neural networks for diabetic retinopathy detection by image classification", Computers & Electrical Engineering, Vol. 72, pp.274-282.

[61] Gargeya R., Leng, T. (2017), "Automated identification of diabetic retinopathy using deep learning", Ophthalmology, Vol. 124(7), pp.962-969.

[62] Xu K., Feng D., Mi, H. (2017), "Deep convolutional neural network-based early automated detection of diabetic retinopathy using fundus image", Molecules, Vol. 22(12), pp.2054.

[63] García G., Gallardo J., Mauricio A., López J., Carpio C.D. (2017), "Detection of diabetic retinopathy based on a convolutional neural network using retinal fundus images", International Conference on Artificial Neural Networks, pp. 635-642.

[64] Pratt H., Coenen F., Broadbent D. M., Harding S. P., Zheng Y. (2016), "Convolutional neural networks for diabetic retinopathy", Procedia Computer Science, Vol. 90, pp.200-205.

[65] B. Antal and A. Hajdu (2012), "An Ensemble-Based System for Microaneurysm Detection and Diabetic Retinopathy Grading", IEEE Transactions on Biomedical Engineering, pages: 1720-1726.

[66] M. Niemeijer, B. van Ginneken, J. Staal, M. S. A. Suttorp-Schulten and M. D. Abramoff (2005), "Automatic detection of red lesions in digital color fundus photographs," in IEEE Transactions on Medical Imaging, vol. 24, no. 5, pp. 584-592.

[67] Tang, L.; Niemeijer, M.; Reinhardt, J.M.; Garvin, M.K. Abramoff, M (2012), "Splat Feature Classification with Application to Retinal Hemorrhage Detection in Fundus Images. IEEE Trans. Med. Imaging, 32, 364–375.

[68] Seoud, L.; Hurtut, T.; Chelbi, J.; Cheriet, F.; Langlois, J.M.P. (2016), "Red Lesion Detection Using Dynamic Shape Features for Diabetic Retinopathy Screening", IEEE Trans. Med. Imaging, vol: 35, 1116–1126.

[69] Prasad, P. (2015), "Retinal hemorrhage detection using feature classification", Int. J. Eng. Comput. Sci., Issue: 4, pp. 10960–10963, 2015.

[70] Haddad, RA & Akansu, (1991), "A class of fast Gaussian binomial filters for speech and image processing", IEEE Transactions on Acoustic speech signal processing, vol.39, pp 723-727.

[71] Fan, R.; Li, X.; Lee, S.; Li, T.; Zhang, H.L. (2020), "Smart Image Enhancement using CLAHE based on an F-Shift Transformation during Decompression", Electronics, Vol.9, pp 1374.

[72] Rashid, M.; Khan, M.A.; Alhaisoni, M.; Wang, S.-H.; Naqvi, S.R.; Rehman, A.; Saba, T. (2020), "A Sustainable Deep Learning Framework for Object Recognition Using Multi-Layers Deep Features Fusion and Selection", Sustainability Vol.12,pp 5037.

[73] Bowling M., Veloso M. (2002), "Multiagent learning using a variable learning rate", Artificial Intelligence, Vol. 136(2), pp.215-250.

[74] Bottou L. (2020), "Stochastic gradient descent tricks", Neural networks: Tricks of the trade, pp. 421-436.

[75] Jyoti Aneja, Aditya Deshpande & Alexander G Schwing (2018), "Convolutional Image Captioning", IEEE/CVF Conference on Computer Vision and Pattern Recognition, pp. 1-10.

[76] Mahmoud, M.H., Alamery, S., Fouad, H., Altinawi, A. and Youssef, A.E. (2021), "An automatic detection system of diabetic retinopathy using a hybrid inductive machine learning algorithm", Personal and Ubiquitous Computing, pp.1-15.

[77] Alabdul wahhab, K.M., Sami, W., Mehmood, T., Meo, S.A., Alasbali, T.A. and Alwadani, F.A. (2021), "Automated detection of diabetic retinopathy using machine learning classifiers", European Review for Medical & Pharmacological Sciences, 25(2).

[78] Wang J., Li, Z. (2018), "Research on face recognition based on CNN", IOP Conference Series: Earth and Environmental Science, Vol. 170(3), pp. 032110.

[79] Li S., Song W., Fang L., Chen Y., Ghamisi P., Benediktsson J.A. (2019), "Deep learning for hyperspectral image classification: An overview", IEEE Transactions on Geoscience and Remote Sensing, Vol. 57(9), pp.6690-6709.

[80] Y. Hou, Y. Cai, Z. Jia, and S. Shi (2020), "Risk factors and prevalence of diabetic retinopathy", Medicine, Vol. 99, No. 42, pp. e22695.

[81] Jadhav A.S., Patil P.B., Biradar S. (2021), "Optimal feature selection-based diabetic retinopathy detection using improved rider optimization algorithm enabled with deep learning", Evolutionary intelligence, Vol. 14(4), pp.1431-1448.

[82] Ali, A., Qadri, S., Khan Mashwani, W., Kumam, W., Kumam, P., Naeem, S., Goktas, A., Jamal, F., Chesneau, C., Anam, S. and Sulaiman, M., (2020), "Machine learning based automated segmentation and hybrid feature analysis for diabetic retinopathy classification using fundus image", Entropy, 22(5), p.567.

[83] Qureshi, I.; Ma, J.; Abbas, Q (2021), "Diabetic retinopathy detection and stage classification in eye fundus images using active deep learning". Multimedia Tools Appl. 80, 11691–11721.

[84] Mumtaz,R.;Hussain, M.; Sarwar, S.; Khan, K.; Mumtaz, S.; Mumtaz, M. (2018), "Automatic detection of retinal hemorrhages by exploiting image processing techniques for screening retinal diseases in diabetic patients", Int. J. Diabetes Dev. Ctries, 38, 80–87.

[85] Semeraro, F, Cancarini, A, Dell Omo,R, Rezzola, S, Romano, MR & Costagliola, C (2015), "Diabetic retinopathy: Vascular and inflammatory disease", Hindawi Publishing Corporation, Journal of Diabetes Research, vol. 2015, pp. 1-16.

[86] Serena Salvatore, Gerald Fishman, A & Mohamed Genead, (2013), "Treatment of cystic macular lesions in hereditary retinal dystrophies", Survey of Ophthalmology, Elsevier, vol. 58, no. 6, pp. 560-584.

[90] Shahid Ahsan, Abdul Basit, Kazi Rumana Ahmed, Liaquat Ali, Fariha Shaheen, Muhammad Saif Ulhaque and Asher Fawwad (2014), "Diagnostic accuracy of direct ophthalmoscopy for detection of diabetic retinopathy using fundus photographs as a reference standard", Diabetes and Metabolic Syndrome: Clinical Research and Reviews, vol. 8, pp. 96-101.

[90] Shobhana, M & Chitrapreyanka, SB (2013), "A novel approach for abnormality detection of macula and fovea region from color fundus images", International Journal of Emerging Trends in Electrical and Electronics, vol. 3, no. 2, pp. 29-35.

[91] Shraddha Tripathi, Krishna Kant Singh, Singh, BK & Akansha Mehrotra (2013), "Automatic detection of exudates in retinal fundus images using differential morphological profile", International Journal of Engineering and Technology, vol. 5, no. 3, pp. 2024-2029.

[92] Siti Syafinah Ahmad Hassan, David Bong, BL & Mallika Premsenthil (2012), "Detection of neovascularization in diabetic retinopathy", Journal of Digital Imaging, Springer, vol. 25, no. 3, pp. 437-444.

[93] Sulaimon Ibrahim, Pradeep Chowriappa, Sumeet Dua, Rajendra Acharya, U, Kevin Noronha, Sulatha Bhandary & Hatwib Mugasa (2015), "Classification of diabetes maculopathy images using data-adaptive neuro-fuzzy inference classifier", Medical and Biological Engineering and Computing, Springer, vol. 53, no. 12, pp. 1345-1360.

[94] Timothy Kern, S & Bruce Berkowitz (2015), "Photoreceptors in diabetic retinopathy", Journal of Diabetes Investigation, Wiley Publications, vol. 6, no. 4, pp. 371-380. 149.

[95] Tomi Kauppi, Joni-Kristian Kamarainen, Lasse Lensu, Valentina Kalesnykiene, Iiris Sorri, Hannu Uusitalo & Heikki Kalviainen (2013), "Constructing benchmark databases and protocols for medical image analysis: Diabetic retinopathy", Hindawi Publishing Corporation Computational and Mathematical Methods in Medicine, vol. 2013,pp. 1-13.

[96] Usman Akram, M & Shoab Khan, A (2013), "Multilayered thresholding based blood vessel segmentation for screening of diabetic retinopathy", Engineering with Computers, Springer, vol. 29, no. 2, pp. 165-173.

[97] Usman Akram, M, Anam Tariq, Shoab Khan, A & Younus Javed, M (2014), "Automated detection of exudates and macula for grading of diabetic macular edema", Computer Methods and Programs in Bio Medicine, Elsevier, vol. 114, no. 2, pp. 141-152.

[98] Usman Akram, M, Shehzad Khalid & Shoab Khan (2013), "Identification and classification of micro aneurysms for early detection of diabetic retinopathy", Pattern Recognition, Elsevier, vol. 46, no. 1, pp. 107-116.

[99] Usman Akram, M, Shehzad Khalid, Anam Tariq & Younus Javed, (2013), "Detection of neovascularization in retinal images using multivariate m-mediods based classifier", Computerized Medical Imaging and Graphics, Elsevier, vol. 37, no. 5-6, pp. 346-357.

[100] Weeagul Pratumgul & Worawat Sa-ngiamvibool (2016), "The prototype of computer-assisted for screening and identifying severity of diabetic retinopathy automatically from color fundus images for mhealth system in Thailand", Procedia Computer Science, Elsevier, vol. 86, pp. 457-460.

[101] Welikala, RA, Fraz, MM, Dehmeshki, J, Hoppe, A, Tah, V, Mann, S, Williamson, TH & Barman (2015), "Genetic algorithm based feature selection combined with dual classification for the automated detection of proliferative diabetic retinopathy", Computerized Medical Imaging and Graphics, Elsevier, vol. 43, pp. 64-77.

[102] Wilfred Franklin, S & Edward Rajan (2014), "Computerized screening of diabetic retinopathy employing blood vessel segmentation in retinal images", Elsevier, Bio cybernetics and Biomedical Engineering, vol. 34, no. 2, pp. 117-124.

[103] Ya-Hsin Kung, Tsung-Tien, Wu & Shwu-Jiuan Sheu 2010, "Subtle solar retinopathy detected by fourier domain optical coherence tomography", Journal of the Chinese Medical Association, vol. 73, no. 7, pp. 396-398.

[104] Yonatan Serlin, Tali Shafat, Jaime Levy, Aaron Winter, Marina Shneck, Boris Knyazer, Yisrael Parmet, Hadar Shalevg, Ehud Ur & Alon Friedman (2016), "Angiographic evidence of proliferative retinopathy predicts neuropsychiatric morbidity in diabetic patients", Psych neuroendocrinology, Elsevier, vol. 67, pp. 163-170.

[105] Young Gun Park & Young-Jung Roh (2015), "New diagnostic and therapeutic approaches for preventing the progression of diabetic retinopathy", Hindawi Publishing Corporation, Journal of Diabetes Research, vol. 2016, pp. 1-10.

[106] Zeinab Ghassabi, Jamshid Shanbehzadeh, Amin Sedaghat & Emad Fatemizadeh (2013), "An efficient approach for robust multimodal retinal image registration based on Ur-SIFT features and PIIFD descriptors", EURASIP Journal on Image and Video Processing, Springer, vol. 2013, no. 25, pp. 1-16.

[107] Zsolt Torok, Tunde Peto, Eva Csosz, Edit Tukacs, Agnes Molnar, M, Andras Berta, Jozsef Tozser, Andras Hajdu, Valeria Nagy, Balint Domokos & Adrienne Csutak(2014), "Combined methods for diabetic retinopathy screening, using retina photographs and tear fluid proteomics biomarkers", Hindawi Publishing Corporation, Journal of Diabetes Research, vol. 2015, pp. 1-8.

www.ingramcontent.com/pod-product-compliance
Lightning Source LLC
LaVergne TN
LVHW082336200926
848481LV00012B/3364